P'91

-2

reduced: 195
1/94 ⊙R⊙ 195

The Second Half of Your Life

The Second Half of Your Life

HOW TO LIVE AND ENJOY IT.

Oren Arnold

Harvest House Publishers
Irvine, California 92714

THE SECOND HALF OF YOUR LIFE

Copyright © 1979 Harvest House Publishers
Irvine, California 92714
Library of Congress Catalog Card Number: 78-65126
ISBN 0-89081-180-6

Printed in the United States of America.

Dedicated

with love to my slightly aging niece

EUGENIA PRESTON PIPSAIRE

for her abiding kindness and enthusiasm, her good humor
and selfless outreach.

THIS AUTHOR—

in extraordinary fashion x-rays your mind, then comes at you with a kind of literary acupuncture.

Already tagged (by the famed psychologist George W. Crane, M.D., Ph.D.) as "America's 20th century Mark Twain," Mr. Arnold verifies here that his needling is not only painless, but is rich in wisdom and subtle charm. His informal friendly reports, his case histories that are perfect for our personal identification, enable him to enrich our spirits in remarkable styling.

With such skill, it is small wonder that he is one of America's most prolific authors. He has published almost 2,000 articles in the major magazines, and more than 80 books—imagine!

Maybe that is all because he was stork-dropped, like the calves and colts, on his parents' big ranch in Texas, when the century was young. Back there you *had* to work hard and be innovative in order to survive.

So now he visits with us delightfully, about what to do with ourselves as *we* age along. His present home and workshop are near Laguna Beach, California, beside the silvery sea. You would be welcome to drop in on him; hundreds do.

—By Gregory T. Mills

Contents

Foreword

No Pampering Here

So now you are middle-aged, or older.

Oh yes you are, if 35 is behind you! Chronologically, the median is 36; emotionally, it can be anywhere between 30 and 50.

In any event, from now on you will operate in a totally new clan, with a chance for developing wisdoms, attitudes and opportunities beyond all imaginings. Mankind's new knowledge guarantees this.

The key warning is—*beware of the future, it is here now.*

It really is. Events have moved so *very* fast that the heralded shock effect is already upon us. As a result, many persons who are "getting along in years" are trying to turn and flee. These end up trembling, cringing, discovering there is no escape. Others put on a front of bravado which, lacking substance, soon deteriorates into self-pity or hostility and cantankerous living, the more abundant life replaced by the moribundant. The older they get, the worse they get. Thus many, many die 20 years or so before they are buried.

But the intelligent ones—at the middle-age crisis point or soon thereafter—quietly take personal inventory, make the proper adjustments, then discover an inspiriting new potential. These perceive that youth, so publicized as alluring and perfect, in reality is often merely an interval of elementary learning, a rather hard prep school, a Time of Trial (there is no escaping clichés on this earth; you think maybe Hereafter?) whereas the *second* half of life can in point of fact be enriched with genuine appreciation and achievement. At least 90 percent of humanity's grandeur has been wrought by persons past 35 years of age; much of it by people past 70.

The objective of this book is to help you with that.

But there shall be no pampering, no coddling; no maunderings about the Good Old Days, no trembly-voiced harking back. This is not a book for the decrepit elderly; it is for the Now people, with alert minds, even though many of these are past 80.

Do expect Truth, in an age of realism. "Grow old along with me, the best is yet to be," is poetic Truth—if! There is no guarantee of it; achieving "the best" is strictly a do-it-yourself project, and it will not be easy. *"Hold fast to your dreams, for if dreams die, life is a broken-winged bird that cannot fly,"* L. Hughes warned us. But the dreams cannot remain vaporous; you must give them substance which they lacked in your youthful years.

The guidance herein is authoritative, gathered from the best modern sources available, not to mention decades of experience and observation. It will be presented as straight informal talk rather than labored literature—just as if you and I were sitting together in a gracious living room before a fireplace on a wintry day, or in the shade of a great oak tree in July. You do not enjoy dull prose, and I try never to write it. Lighthearted, friendly style does not imply light weight in importance.

Come along . . .

O.A.

1

Adaptability
The All-Important New Theme
Of Our Lives

When you arrived on this earth your very first action was one of protest.

For months you had lived in luxury; no responsibilities, no conscience to nag you, no food to buy, no taxes, complete security, no problems. The perfect situation. You "had it made."

Then all at once you felt a slap on your bottom, you gulped in some strange substance that you had never even dreamed existed, you felt the impact of light and sound—and you howled. You had been enjoying a stable environment, when in one frightening moment your situation radically changed.

Such is the first great shock that human beings face. The psychologists tell us that our benign period in the womb does indeed put into each of us a *resistance to change*, which tends to increase as we age along. It has been that way since Adam awoke and discovered Eve. He was shocked at the thought that he would now have to *adapt*. Something New had appeared in the Garden; there was no longer a comfortable, dependable status quo.

True, you have been aware of "change" for many years; of newness on the world scene and in your personal life. But for a long, long time it was—shall we say—trivial? You voiced a protest, you howled about it, just as you did at your borning; we all did. But we accepted it, rather ungraciously. Then we all scowled and told one another that "times change" and "things aren't the same anymore" and made endless similar trite summations.

Truth is—things did change, but at a rather set, predictable, acceptable pace, giving us time to accept and somehow go along without too much mental disturbance. For hundreds of thousands of years—the experts tell us—the sum total of human knowledge, everything that man knew about everything on earth, was doubling about once every 100 years. This lasted until somewhere near the turn into the 20th century A.D.

But then—dear God!—in just 50 or 60 years, which is a bare snap of the fingers as time has to be measured, the sum total of human knowledge was doubling every *five* years!

That is the most important fact of this century.

That is also the most powerful and influential fact in the lives of present-day people in the second half of their lives.

That sudden acceleration in mankind's acquisition of new knowledge, has scared the unholy bejabbers out of us aging citizens; meaning, generally, anybody past 35 years of age. The shock of it seems worse than the effect of that first gulp of air when we emerged from the womb. The status quo? Hah—it has evaporated. "What was good enough for my old father is good enough for me?" Impossible! Absolutely nothing seems fixed or dependable anymore. And we aging folk are howling in protest, as vehemently as we howled back there in the delivery room.

As never before in human history, newness is a positive, powerful *Force*.

Its impact on humanity is beyond measuring, though you may not yet have recognized this. It's just as if, say, you had been dozing in the backseat of your sedan (itself a kind of womb) and now you awaken to discover that your teenage grandson at the wheel has revved the car up from 55 miles per hour to 550! This is the "Future Shock" sort of thing so graphically thrown at us a few years ago by author Alvin Toffler. That "future" is now here. And what we do about it can make or break our lives. I now declare to you that a totally new adaptability is imperative, as the day to day theme of our existence. It is also the basic theme of this book.

SOME SPECIFIC "FOR-INSTANCES"

To make the matter clear, let's drop generalities and list a few specifics, getting right down to the nitty-gritty personal impact of change and newness:

1. Our alarm that ranks Number 1 in intensity is *galloping inflation*.

Youth tends to shrug it off or even grin at it, in supreme confidence. Perhaps they are right, but we aging folks do not think so. Especially do those of us past age 60 all too well "remember when." The horrors of 1930 remain vivid in our memories. We also recall that in all of human history, in any nation, no big monetary inflation has ever ended in anything except a fall over the cliff, with all the attendant tragedy and panic.

That of course sounds harshly pessimistic. Is it, forsooth, just the trembly-voiced maundering of old men and women? I pray just the trembly-voiced maundering of old men and women? I pray to God that it is! I pray that we are wrong. By nature I am an optimist; I *do* have "faith," both in God and country. Yet it has always seemed that "faith" must inevitably be undergirded with caution and common sense. The Bible says so, in a hundred ways. Experience and observation verify it. Maybe our vaunted New Knowledge can indeed come up with a plan that will reverse inflation, and save us. Most assuredly, dear Lord, I pray for *that!* Moreover, I'll be cow-kicked if somewhere back in my inner consciousness I don't predict it! I just can't force myself to envision another devastating national financial bust-up. Congress or the President or *somebody* will come up with a solution. Probably it will be many somebodys; the whole body politic, good old vox populi himself, I feel so because it—he—has an immense goodness, plus all this additional modern know-how. In 1930 America simply didn't have intelligence enough to control a panicky depression. Today, maybe we do have.

Meanwhile, our universal old-age concern about inflation

is best symbolized by—

a. The cost of gasoline. We resent having to pay 80 cents or more for a gallon, when just yesterday (as recently as 1971) it was 16 cents or less. We have every reason to think that we have been "had;" that the petroleum corporations—or somebody—has been exploiting us. Our indignation about this extends right on through all of merchandising—food, clothing, housing, health care for sure, everything.

b. Services. Virtually every citizen over age 40 reacts with anger or impatience when we go into a store and find few if any clerks to wait on us or even answer questions.

Oh yes, we have come to accept the big self-serve supermarket grocery stores. But we still resent having to paw through acres of space at Sears, Penny's, Wards and other huge department stores, trying—on our own—to locate the counter for underwear, and even there locate our favorite brand name, size and style, then carry it half a block indoors to a rather indifferent and even disdainful cashier. We scowl at such treatment. What is this world coming to? We grew up having courteous store managers and clerks to wait on us, and in our own stores we served our customers with consideration and personal concern. Today even a plumber—paid outrageously at up to $100 or more per *hour* (a verified fact)—may promise to come this morning and show up next week if at all.

These service situations are closely tied to inflation, of course. History shows that the only cure for arrogance in service and selling is—hunger. When we need them, they become arrogant; when they need *us,* for their own survival—hoo boy! Then, again, the customer will be king. That's the way it was in the 1930's; the president of the busted bank coming penniless to our doors eager to sell us an apple for a nickel or to mow our lawn for 50 cents. Precisely that happened. It could happen again, and we old ones know it.

One more for instance—

2. The music of today—if music it is—infuriates us.

We oldsters grew up on hearts-and-flowers melodies that

were—well, dang it all—melodious! Singable. Hummable. Whistleable. Having to do with the moon in June beside the lagoon where we could croon and spoon. My beautiful teen-age sister Opal—who lived well past 80 and is now in heaven, thank You, Lord—in 1915 deftly and happily coaxed such melodies out of our old upright piano in the parlor of our Texas farm and ranch home. Young people from nearby Town loved to gather there—and sing. Mother herself might start it off, harking back to her own youth—

"Beautiful dream-ER-R-R
Come unto me-e-eeee—"

and for an encore maybe she would do *Jeannie With The Light Brown Hair*, and the young folk would join her, heart-touched by Stephen Foster. Then likely all would switch to that really "modern" and slightly daring

"Come on and hear
Come on and hear
Alexander's ragtime band."

Our mother never quite knew just what "ragtime" meant, nor did we, but she at least suspected that it held some kind of off-color connotation, thereby conflicting with her Presbyterian heritage. This was verified when we—in her absence from the parlor—would daringly slip into—

"O-o-o-o-o-o you beautiful dol-l-l-l
You great big beautiful dol-l-l-l-l
Le-e-e-et me put my arms around you—"

Heavens, probably mama had a point! We young folks would blush at our own temerity; we were feeling our oats. But we nevertheless were singing in lilting lyrics, and on tedious Monday afternoons I could sing that way in my saddle rounding up cattle, or in the great lonesome fields when I was plowing corn.

Today, we oldsters reflect that all such niceness went out with boys' short haircuts. Nobody sings at work anymore. Nobody whistles happily, trudging down a country lane to bring home the milk cows. Nobody strolls hand-in-hand with a sweetheart and croons beside a lagoon. Bing Crosby himself became old and died, and at this writing Rudy Vallee is wrinkled and gray.

That wonderful old moonlight-and-roses music has been replaced by a cacaphony of drums and a raucous whanging of electric guitars, accompanying wildly discordant mating calls in monotonous off-key tones, all in high-count decibels that hammer the ear drums and insure deafness by middle age. (Ask any otologist).

"Good" or "bad" is not the consideration here. It's just that we oldsters feel sorry for the modern younger degeneration. We are quite certain that they don't know what they are missing, and this disturbs all of us to no end.

All right, the point is made.

We could list a thousand for-instances. We recognize that change is inevitable, and that we as individuals have to do much of the changing.

The degree to which we adapt, will determine whether or not the remaining years of our life are the best of all. I can tell you, authoritatively, that the elders of America *are* adapting to all this newness, fighting the bad parts of it, encouraging the endless good parts. This is rapidly creating a unified social, political and economic unit, aging men and women who not only have intelligence but also *now* have the wisdom that only intelligence and experience together can bring. Truly, we are the Emerging Elders.

In effect, we are serving notice again, right now. The aging folk are taking over, 35 to 40 million of us emerging to save America from its follies. We are led not by wrinkled rheumy-eyed patriarchs with cracked voices, but mostly by middle-aged gents and gals who still have an abundance of energy. They are the modern Decision Makers, leading us in a second American Revolution. For the freeloaders hiding behind tenure or exploiting their fellow men, it is a sociological and economic Armageddon, and they are doomed to lose.

If you are past 35 and have a crumb of decency in you, get into the action!

2

The Future Has Arrived!

But Please Don't Panic

The automobile of the year 2000 will have no steering wheel.

If you wish to travel from your home to that of your daughter 400 miles away, you will step inside the car, press buttons that match her zip code, street and house numbers, and one that says START. Within four hours you will stop gently at your daughter's door.

En route, you may lie down and sleep, sit and read, play bridge, listen to music, enjoy television along with hot food and drink from the car's own heater or cold from its freezer. Your motor will be silent, fission powered along a metal guide strip embedded in the pavement, with safety guaranteed by radar.

You don't believe it?

Neither do I. But then—you and I are old fogeys. Our minds are grooved; conditioned by horse-and-buggy thinking. Matter of fact, I am old enough to have hitched up many a horse and buggy, earning a dime for it when my older brothers wanted to go off courting girls in 1912 to 1920 or so. No indeed, my mentality cannot emcompass driverless automobiles.

On the other hand, good sense tells me that we will all have to adapt to them. Facts, in whatever form, cannot be avoided. At about middle age the human mind does tend to become fixed—on what has been, instead of what is going to be. The sociologists tell us that an estimated half the population is like that. Which is why we have so many traditionalists, or conservatives. These tend to hark back, often taking an unctuous pride in the way their parents lived and thought. From this group, come the avid seekers of "antiques," and the folks who go in heavily for history and folklore, and the couples who like to buy an old ramshackle mansion or even a barny country house and "restore" it. Tacitly these say they are supporting the Eternal Verities—whatever *those* are! A great many of them belong to the Republican Party. Some of them collect vintage automobiles. Most of them make a point of dressing themselves with restraint which they refer to as Good Taste in Clothes, their manners are impeccable even though rather stuffy, they belong to the Classics Book Club, they attend lectures.

And they sit around asking one another what is this world coming to! This is often called the age-40 syndrome, and it can get worse as the years pass. They look askance at the liberals, the rather slaphappy or uninhibited set in the loud Hawaiian shirts and skirts, who listen to rock music and do some hang gliding and build modernistic homes with glass roofs and solar-energy machines.

Neither group is any "better" than the other!

It's just that the liberals, the more casual don't-give-a-hoot-what-happens clan at middle age, find that acceptance of change is not only easy but also is a pleasure. It's harder on the others.

You individually have to decide which group is yours. Perhaps the ideal is somewhere in between the two; the person who can cherish the best from the past; anticipate the future with eagerness, and enjoy the present with marked enthusiasm and zest.

The happiest factor is that the two groups get along with each other fine. Oh yes, a few snobs develop in each group; but nobody—except themselves—takes them seriously; we Americans are truly a tolerant people, we don't often get mad at one another because one doesn't think like the other.

Gerald Ford and Jimmy Carter, representing the two factions politically, remained cordial friends after their famous campaign for the Presidency; in America the new President never has his rival shot at sunrise, he invites him to the White House for dinner, and even consults him on matters of national importance.

IS THE POINT CLEAR?

So then, don't feel badly if you have been guilty of resisting change. Because, dearly beloved, *you yourself can change!*

If you are ultra-conservative and old-fashioned, you will have to!

Go ahead, collect your vintage automobiles, for fun. But keep in mind that the upcoming models will have no steering wheels, and that this will be a marked advance. Is the point clear?

Actually, we may not even have many ground cars at all. Experts tell us that most of our travel in the year 2000 likely will be in the air: freight trains zipping through the skies, along with luxury passenger liners up there, coast to coast in 20 minutes! And around town, from home to "the office" or the job? In *hovercraft!* That's a smallish one-person or two-person vehicle about the size and shape of a telephone booth, inexpensive, electronically controlled, to land you at the supermarket or near your place of work.

Such news is shocking, isn't it? Well, so was the crossbow; it was going to destroy humanity, when it first appeared; the Pope himself said so! So do not scowl, do not be skeptical. Accept; and prepare to adapt. Take the inevitable in stride.

Consider now the telephone, which is probably the most taken-for-granted miracle of our century. Before 1990 it will be about the size of a pack of cigarettes. It will be worn on your belt or on your wrist, or in the woman's purse. No wires. When you want to talk to your friend in, say, California or Calcutta or Seattle or Sydney, just touch tiny number buttons. Instantly the signal will leap from you to Telstar to

Telstar to another phone on your friend's wrist, anywhere on earth or in the skies. Incidentally, the number you call will also be your friend's Social Security number, insurance number, street address number, on and on; each person will have just *one* number to nurse along—a godsend!

Your distant friend will hear a ting or a bleep, look at his wrist gadget, see your portrait in 3-dimension 4-color perfection, and you will see his. Assured identification. A personal visit, as you converse casually in normal routine. Moreover, the same telephone will also tell you the time, speaking it aloud every five minutes or quarter-hour, as you wish. And show you the month, year, day, hour and second, and will have a reminder alarm as needed. It will all cost you less than $20 plus maybe a dollar or two per month, and require almost no service for repairs.

Impossible?

Unbelievable?

Phooey, we are already doing that! Give us just a few years to replace all our present horse-and-buggy telephone equipment.

Truth is, we are already using much similar technical know-how in communications. For instance, three regional editions of the eminent *Wall Street Journal*, a highly respected daily newspaper, are printed instantaneously and electronically by facsimile pages shot from Chicopee Falls, Mass., into the skies for more than 20,000 miles thence back to receivers separated by hundreds of miles across the USA. All those costly cumbersome Linotypes and grinding wheels in pressrooms of newspapers are doomed for the junk heap. Very soon your private newspaper will roll into your living room from a gadget much like your television set, all day and all night if you wish it to, and will be illuminated on the TV screen itself if you prefer. All of this will discombobulate the neighbor boy who today has perfected the art of tossing the evening journal onto your roof or behind the thorny hedges. But then somebody always suffers in the path of progress.

Now do not freeze up at me, don't get mad. These things, I repeat, are feasible NOW; we just can't make the change-over instantaneously. But by the year 1990—broth-er! Communications will make our present-day processes look like Pony Express efforts. Yes, prepare your mind to accept and adapt; "times" are changing.

GET TRANQUILIZED,
THEN READ ON
Right here, best pop a Valium pill or other brain bender into your gullet so that you won't react with violence or fear. Because I have even more startling communication news for you, more Tofflerian "future shock" phenomena which are fast arriving.

That fancy wrist or belt telephone may not in fact arrive at all. Because—get a good grip on yourself here—the phenomenon of thought transference seems to be in the immediate offing.

Thought transference!
Good heavens, what is that?

Well, dearly beloveds, it means that my wife can tell what I am thinking when I am 2 miles or 200 miles or 2000 miles away from her. And I'm not sure I like that!

Surely you know a bit about electricity. Plus the fact that electric or *some* kind of waves emanate constantly from every human being, just as they do from certain eels and other creatures, and that information rides those waves. I have a big fine poodle dog named Pepe le Moku. He sleeps under my desk as I work at my typewriter, with my shoeless feet resting on his fur. But—just let my wife Adele—whom he loves dearly—get through heavy traffic within half a mile of our home, and Pepe leaps up, scratches on the door to get out and run to meet her. He is in the driveway when she turns her car in. Somehow, by some mysterious means, that pooch knows she is coming, when there is no possible way for him to hear or smell her or her car in a welter of traffic out there. How? I have no idea; I only work here. But such is a common phenomenon. Obviously from Adele come some of these unseen unheard emanations or "waves" which tell Pepe something.

E.S.P. AND PRE-COGNITION

Now hear this: today our parapsychologists and other research scientists are learning how to identify, control and direct those emanations from human beings, to carry information from one person's brain to another's. There are many new records of successful thought transference. Extrasensory perception is not just a dream.

Pause and re-read that. Try to absorb it. Distance seems not to be a factor. Interference seems not to be. Certain people under certain conditions can swap thought over 24 feet or over 24,000 miles—which is the circumference of the earth. Some very reliable and honest people even have *pre*-cognition; they "see" things happening next Friday or next week or next month, and by jiminy they happen precisely as foreseen. Typically, Mrs. Wallis Mogg, a devout Episcopalian lady, housewife and mother, has foreseen events weeks ahead. In each instance she went quietly to her vicar who made note of her mental images. And the events developed precisely at the times and places she had envisioned. The parapsychology clinic of research laboratory at Duke University, under the famous Dr. Rhine, got onto that. So, "thought"—or awareness, or knowledge, or whatever—can be and is being transferred right here in our time.

I agree; I don't believe it either.

I hitched horses to buggies, and marveled at that fantastically impossible new contraption, the telephone. How could the human voice *possibly* travel along a thin wire—dear God! The wire wasn't even hollow, as a speaking tube might be. So—a miracle. Magic. Mystery.

When radio came along my papa, who had been born during the Civil War, was greatly distressed. The transmission of dots and dashes by wire was astonishing enough, but by wireless—heavens! It somehow seemed sinful. Or at least

supernatural. It even smacked of witchcraft, or something—
how well I remember the talk of those times. But when papa
lived to see television—God bless his old-man grandeur, he
had adapted. He took TV in stride. Even though still
appalled and excited and ignorant about it, he accepted it as
a major advance. Can I be that open-minded? I'm trying.
Can you be?

No, I do not "believe in" Thought Transference. I don't
believe in the color television action pictures coming in absolute perfection into my living room. I don't believe it because
I don't understand it, such miracles leave me loopy in the
mind. *Thought Transference!* Good jumping jupiter what
won't they think up next, these young hepcat children and
grandchildren of ours, taking such events for granted here in
the Spage Age? I feel weak. I think I will go lie down and
pray. I hitched up horses and buggies.

AS IF THAT WEREN'T ENOUGH

But the next exhibit here gets us to something infinitely
more exciting. The prognosticators (I try never to use a short
word when a long one will do) envision something else. It
too is based on electrical or some other kind of "waves." The
waves that strike our eyeballs, say, from a football game, go
out in a positive sphere *ad infinitum*. Meaning, they do not
disintegrate, they just go on and on, and on, for thousands,
millions, billions of light years. Okay?

Moreover, if they hit something, they bounce.

They "echo" or come back to us, as the beam of a flash-
light does when shone on a mirror. All we need to do is build
a receiving set that will pick them up and put them on our
TV screens in sharp focus again—*and we are close to learning
how to do that*.

Thus in a few more years, the experts insist, we will have
what they call Time Restoration.

By catching light waves that are bouncing back to us from
distant planets and such, we earthlings will be able actually to
see the Crucifixion, the destruction of Pompeii, the Battle of

Bunker Hill, the Inauguration of Abraham Lincoln. We will have a Time TV Set, with channels to catch that light bounce.

Now now, again I plead with you, do not get mad or sneer and act cynical. What would the witchcraft people have done to Benjamin Franklin if he had predicted television, or to Abe Lincoln for that matter? We don't dare be skeptical. We have to weave with such news, or the second half of our lives will be sheer misery.

THE ULTIMATE SHOCK

But all of the above is really only a mental warmup toward accepting this next prediction. Relatively little about this one has been published anywhere, because any talk about it would seriously disturb simple-minded people. I am gambling that you who read this book are *not* simple minded, but are willing at least to consider almost anything at all, and stay open-minded.

This one comes, as of now, from the realm of probability only. But it is an esoteric-scientific-spiritual thrust of new knowledge that will be the ultimate shocker, so hold on tight and do not rock the boat.

Within the next few years—maybe 20, maybe 50, not likely more—PEOPLE ALIVE ON EARTH WILL BE ABLE TO COMMUNICATE HAPPILY WITH PEOPLE WHO ARE DEAD.

As I said—stay calm. Keep an open mind.

There is no proof as of today; nothing that any learned body of men or women declares to be absolute fact. But parapsychologists and other intensely dedicated, educated, honest, quiet, capable researchers declare that we are on the threshold!

With little that is yet precise or concrete or blueprinted or guaranteed, their instincts nevertheless are zinging like taut strings on a banjo—which for any researcher is always a warning that something BIG is about to happen. They have a— a *feeling!* Intuitive awareness, the kind that nearly always presages success. We will soon be able to communicate with our loved ones who have preceded us to the afterlife.

"But I am atheist," you may declare. "All such talk as that is pure hogwash."

Maybe it is. *Maybe*. But keep this in mind, Buster or Bertha: in this enlightened era, atheists are an obfuscated minuscule minority. (Hoo boy, what luscious polysyllabification that is!) I doubt if there are 10,000 genuine atheists in North America. Truth is, *any* atheist is revealing the most colossal of all conceits. He is saying that he is smarter than 99 percent of all the kings and queens and presidents of earth, the distinguished scientists, philosophers, statesmen, scholars, industrial leaders, the truly gifted and creative thinkers at all levels, and surely of the millions of humbler people.

A few who do believe in God will be outraged at the thought of ever communicating with people in the spirit world. "That's blasphemy," these may cry out.

I can understand that reaction. We wise old folk cannot be taken in by such charlatans, can we? No. We have lived. We know what's what; let nobody try to make fools of us.

But then—I remember seeing my very first airplane. Paid a whole dollar to get into a cow pasture to see it take off in flight. But it wouldn't go, and the poor pilot—who was trying to earn money for further research in aeronautics—had to give us our dollars back. We razzed him and all his kind, saying there in 1912 that if God had meant for man to fly we would have been given wings. Such was the standard comeback, the ultimate put-down, of that decade.

But some erudite gent there said we were wrong. He declared that the time would come, very likely in this 20th century, too, when men *would* fly in airplanes; and not just a few yards like the Wright brothers did, but all the way from our town of Henderson to big Dallas, Texas, a distance of 120 miles. Imagine!

Well, of course, that man was a crackpot, to be pitied. So from the superiority of my then 12 years I pontificated that "Man has about as much chance of ever flying from here to

Dallas, as he'd have of ever flying to the moon."

Believe me, that told 'em, that squelched the optimist, and everybody smiled. I gained great status among my peers, and even the superintendent of schools told the listeners there that afternoon that Oren Arnold was a bright boy. Dear God!

NOTHING IS "IMPOSSIBLE"

We do have some concrete information about that business of dying. There have been not one or two but many instances of persons declared physically and legally dead, some of them for several minutes, who revived and reported in detail about their discoveries on the "other side." Fascinating!

In fact there is a whole new book about such scientific-spiritual phenomena, and it it has been highly acclaimed as authentic, plausible—and exciting. It's title is *Life After Life,* by Raymond A. Moody, Jr., M.D. It was condensed in the magazine that has had the greatest impact on the human race of anything ever published except the Bible—*The Reader's Digest.* I well know from experience how meticulous the *Digest* editors are about accuracy, how they forced me to verify and prove every detail of the many articles I have written for them.

The most wonderful aspect of Dr. Moody's report is—the people who admitted to having been "dead" then returning to mortal life, unanimously declared that existence after what we call death was altogether delightful.

Paradise? What they found was literally that; no, figuratively, for "paradise" is a variable. Reared among amiable psalm-singing Negroes, I long ago developed a mental picture of Heaven as a city with streets and houses of glistening solid gold, entered through arched gates of literal pearl, with me hugged in welcome there by my mother and Saint Peter and Jesus Christ. Today, I realize that to many people on earth "heaven" is enough food to eat and a pair of shoes. But the whole of those "dead" persons' experience is that it was more than good, Dr. Moody reports; it was extremely heartening to all of us who have so assiduously nursed our fears and hopes.

I do not know *how* our brainy folk will develop communication with the dead. They postulate that it may have something to do with those electrical or other emanations, those "waves" we discussed, mysterious forces which we do not yet understand and cannot define. A miracle? What is a miracle? Whenever man does anything "impossible" it is hailed as a miracle, and he has done that a billion times. The wheel was a miracle. Taming the horse to hitch to the wheel was a miracle. The steamship, the telegraph, the automobile, the telephone, all were miracles; you well know.

Right here, I could list a hundred new ones. For further example—there is a new sheet plastic which will not allow either heat or cold to go through it. Fancy that! Wrap a bit of it around your hand, turn a blow torch on it, and you feel nothing. Make a tent of it in Prudhoe Bay, Alaska, at minus 60 degrees F. in February, then sleep in with only one pad on the hard earth and you in light pajamas. Impossible! A miracle! But just think what that means in the realm of fabrics and insulation.

Another one—our scientists have developed a chemical which, sprayed on wood or cloth or anything at all, makes it absolutely fireproof! Which means that, as soon as we can get the stuff into production and distributed, destructive fires should be forever ended.

No, don't you dare say we *won't* ever do *anything*.

"Change" is upon us; newness, with all that the word connotes.

No, everything "new" today is not good; certainly not. But the adaptability on which I keep harping, is not at all the same as mere blind *acceptance*. If something obviously is "bad"—fight it! Reject it. Destroy it. Crime on the streets, for example. Sexual freedom, for example, flaunting the great Commandment about adultery. We who are the Emerging Elders have an obligation to be choosy, to be selective; but not to be critical or afraid. Never! Almost literally any desirable advance, any new knowledge, today is at least conceivable, day-dreamable; especially if you are young minded and alert.

Come to think about it—what DO you anticipate? What do you envision as Progress? How much adapting and refocusing are you prepared to do?

What is the substance of your earthly yearnings?

If there were dreams to sell . . . *what would you buy?*

3

Forestall The
Moribundant Life

For most women and men who have turned the midpoint of aging, the most prevalent "dream"—which is to say, the focusing of their desires—is for that rather vaguely defined routine called The Abundant Life.

These have conditioned their minds to think that if they could just have enough money, enough worldly goods, enough "things" in literal abundance, earthly perfection would be achieved. Challenged and questioned about it, most also would say that, yes, yes we want "abundance" in the intangible as well; respect, even deference, from neighbors and business associates; social status, well above mere acceptance; respect for their mentalities and good judgment and astuteness in all areas.

The sum of all that is equated with "Success."

You will note that no mention was made of physical, mental, emotional and spiritual health. But on second thought—yes indeed, they want those too! Such folk invariably smile wryly and admit that—well, actually, of course, we think those psychic or inner values should come first.

But the implication is that any mention of them is superfluous; is in fact not quite the expected or proper thing to do. In our modern materialistic culture, it simply is old-fashioned, even a bit childish, to discuss such concepts in quick-witted sophisticated society.

It is precisely this tacit attitude—an almost universal "dream"—which has backfired in recent years. The dream has turned into a nightmare.

Psychologically, the net result is that millions of folks at middle age and older have consciously or unconsciously developed not a more abundant but a *mori*bundant life.

Moribund! The dictionary definition of it is dying, or coming to an end. And such is precisely the feeling a vast number of good-hearted, well intentioned, but now suddenly desperate men and women are developing as they consciously turn "middle age." Perhaps this is the most heartening aspect of the newness and change on the North American and world scene.

THE DREAM GOES "BLIP!"

Formerly, that routine of self-delusion began to wane at about age 50. In recent years, it has been striking in the late 30s and early 40s. The awakening begins as a quiet realization, a new wondering and questioning, a rather pitiful searching, progressing into anxiety then fear. Suddenly the dream goes "blip!" and we awake in figurative darkness. So here we are—"aging" even old, and our first potentially grand fruitful years seem now to have been wasted.

There is indeed something alarming about that awakening. Thus many of us feel that we are now on the downhill toward death, or at best a miserable old age. Moreover, if we aren't careful we will tell our associates about that *ad nauseam*.

This critical and chronic display of self-pity quickly becomes intolerable. You can no longer take the high hurdles as you see the teens and the 20s and the 30s doing, so you conclude that you are done, licked, defeated, on the skids of life. and indeed you are—if you persist in that! Self-pity is the worst form of cancer; it destroys the psyche, the self-respect, the soul. Even undue grief very soon degenerates into self-pity if we allow it; my mate is gone, whatever am I going to do, who is going to take care of me? Me, me, me, I, I, I. The first-person-singular soon crowds everything else out of your moribund brain.

So?

So, to cope with the newly surging life in America, it is

apparent that persons of middle age and older must develop a totally new set of attitudes. That truth is repeated here for emphasis. If the second half of your life is going to have any zest and satisfaction at all, an upgraded attitude is your Number 1 priority. It is the very essence of "adapting."

A NEW APPROACH TO RELIGION

The most important New Attitude for the 1980s probably is that one having to do with religion.

The very word "religion" all too often is bandied about, carelessly used and misused, and thus has lost any really sharp definition for millions of folk who are middle-aged or older.

But the strong fact of the matter is, in America (also in Canada, England, Australia and many other nations) "religion" remains virtually synonymous with "Christianity."

If you are Jewish, please do not take umbrage. (One of these fine days I am going to take time to look up "umbrage" in the dictionary. Meanwhile *you* look it up. It's an old-fashioned word which I think means to get your hackles up, get spittin' mad, or similar . . . Where was I? . . . Oh yes—). Or even if you are Mohammedan or Confucionist or Buddist—or, forsooth, atheistic, which is unlikely—do not react here with indignation. Religious freedom is still one of America's Great Four (can you name the other three?). Certainly there is no ill will toward any of you. It's just that, statistically, the vast majority of Anglo-Saxons are at least nominal followers of Christ.

Among the mature-minded ones of these, is the feeling that the Good News of the gospels remains as the best good news the world has ever received. For us, this amounts to a stability, a rock-like foundation for our lives; one of the concepts that modern knowledge has *not* changed. Most of this group feel that we do not need to change our attitude toward our religion.

But hark—

Our *dissemination* of that Good News is rapidly changing,

and well it should. It is here, in this aspect of the matter, that our attitudes toward religion have to be flexible.

This absolutely does *not* require any compromise with conscience.

The Ten Commandments, for instance, have not been declared unconstitutional. (In fact it is said that humanity has passed ten million laws trying to enforce them.)

The Psalms still sing out their divine promises of glory and grandeur, reassurance and hope.

The Sermon on The Mount is as magnificent as it was when first delivered.

The miracles that Christ performed have not lost their awe for us, because we see comparable miracles in our time.

It was he who activated the greatest word in our English language—tenderness; and here 2,000 years later our most modern psychiatrists and psychologists describe tenderness as the indispensable emotion. (As a word, "love" has come into too much careless misuse, hence no longer ranks first.)

You can feel at ease, therefore, in your attitude toward the Holy Bible. It is not going out of date. Indeed almost every month there is a big new edition of it, with new translations that speak to us with unprecedented clarity and beauty, changing not the truths but simply updating the idiom.

That is a part of what I meant by changes in dissemination of Christian teaching. Updating it. Using modern language—changing thee and thy to you and your, for example—in direct pulpit confrontation and personal contacts.

THE "ELECTRIC CHURCH"

But there's more.

In the Olden Days (prior to 1920 or so) Christianity was spread primarily by word of mouth, person to person. That is still the best way, but its efficiency is limited. So today we have what *The Wall Street Journal* calls "The Electric Church," coming right into our homes, our boats and ships and automobiles, by air from distinguished evangelists and others. Hundreds of radio stations, and dozens of television stations, now broadcast worship services, music, sermons, guidance, prayers, on weekdays as well as Sundays. As of this writing, a new radio station is joining them at the rate of one a week, and TV stations once a month. Enough money pours in from the listeners to more than pay the costs, so grateful are the multitudes.

Do you dare disapprove of all that?

Are you so tradition bound that you react with indignation, so "set in your ways" that you cannot change?

Jesus used the public relations techniques of his time. So aren't we obligated to use the best ones of our era? (See the new book titled *Holy Ballyhoo, Effective Publicity For Your Church;* C,S,S, Publishing Co.)

We today have many wonderful new books interpreting the Bible for us and teaching us how to apply it in our daily routine, in a clarity never before enjoyed. Also there are many new church-related magazines, newspapers, pamphlets. In short, we have superb new *guidance* and help in developing an updated attitude toward the national religion; a blessing that our grandparents never enjoyed.

If you decry the use of these modern methods and media—shame on you. Your attitude is still horse-and-buggy here in the Jet Age. Christianity is flourishing as never before, while you try to remain rigidly authoritarian and insist on the Old Ways. But you can't win! You can never argue with success. So, readjust your pride. Change your attitude and shout "Hallelujah!"

Just be sure you keep in mind that Christianity is not a passive self-centered do-nothing religion. It is true that Christians sit in church for instructions. They do sit briefly together for prayers and guidance. They do take time to rest at home and meditate. Then they get up and get going! They subscribe to that warning in the fine old spiritual which says "You will never get to heaven in a rocking chair." Too many thousands of people start rocking and shirking—goofing off?—when they turn age 35 or 40 or so; which is stupid of them.

The very word "church" has changed in meaning. For many centuries it was associated with a specific building. Christ himself often made his way into the temples, to worship and preach and teach and heal. We moderns have but to visit Rome or Paris or Milan or that compact mother-of-America, England, to see ancient and awesome cathedrals, still in use. Their cost in materials, manpower and maintenance is beyond reckoning, and they are still in use. But my Adele and I have repeatedly visited them, and each time have come out depressed because *we never saw more than one-tenth of their seats filled at worship services.*

Never mind all the psychological theories as to why they are so little used, except as tourist attractions. Just know that the disuse does NOT imply any decline in religious fervor. It simply means that new methods of "advertising" the Good News have come into vogue. We do not have to crawl on our knees for half a mile to some architectural pile, in order to cleanse our souls (though this is still done in some places). We do not require gargoyles and saints and scrolls on high masonry walls held upright by flying buttresses, in order to sense the majesty and grandeur of God as millions of our ancestors did. And that itself is good news.

OUR MODERN AWARENESS

Which means that we in Europe and America are now focusing—as never before—on subtler realities of Christianity, as distinguished from the physical symbolic aspects. That magnificent cathedral in Milan, for instance, still has enormously heavy bells that frighten the tourists more than they inspire the worshippers. All of us respect those architectural wonders; but generally, here in our Jet Age, we ascribe them to a rather misguided past, while we reach out for a much deeper, richer proclamation of Christianity. There is a new awareness, everywhere, among Catholics and Protestants alike. Many Catholics are challenging even their Pope, still loving him but seeing him no longer as a God incarnate but simply as a devout member of human society elected to lead them. Similarly, the Protestants no longer cringe or get flustered when the Presbyterian or the Baptist or the Methodist pastor calls; he is merely The Reverend Doctor Somebody, one of us, who has headaches and arthritis and troublesome children and dandelions on his lawn and high taxes and indigestion, just as we do, needing our help and guidance as much as we need his.

Compared to, say, 1880, this is all a totally new attitude among citizens everywhere, meaning people past 35. If you who read here have not developed it—could it be that you are rather behind the times?

This newness is further pointed up by significant changes in the patterns of worship themselves, especially among Protestants. True, many of our churches still are very "fundamental," thinking there is merit in worshipping only in the manner of our ancestors. But a vast new generation of young folk—teenagers, adults in their 20s or turning into early 30s—have quietly revolutionized that thinking. Thus today we often have guitars and banjos twanging in our sanctuaries on a Sabbath morning, accompanied by rhythmic hand clapping, and marching around, and banner carrying, and folk singing, and often even some form of dancing, all this in addition to spoken testimonies and prayers.

Many thousands of such services now are held in homes, in outdoor patios, at the beach, under spreading trees, in city parks, at the lakeshore, on college campuses, almost anywhere at all, even in prison cells. There are almost 600,000 ordained ministers in America, and most of them do *not* have conventional church buildings. Can you realize the importance of this?

After all, what precisely *is* "worship?"

Who is to say that it must be exactly thus and so? Rigidity about it is untenable, no matter what your heritage may be, or the tradition in your community, or the sect to which you belong. In Arizona, modern Hopi Indians worship God— believe it or not—by dancing outdoors while holding live, poisonous rattlesnakes in their hands and mouths! This is in late 20th century America, mind you, not in "darkest heathen Africa" or other remote jungle area.

I agree with you that it is inconceivable. But I also warn you not to develop an attitude of intolerance just because you have reached middle age or older. There are endless variants in worship, so just you be wary lest the world run away from you and leave you, alone, crying frantically in the wilderness.

FERVIDLY? OR FERVENTLY?

To avoid moribundancy in daily routine, the overall most important assessment that you as a modern aging citizen must make is this:

Am I working, planning, playing and living in a frantic, fervid manner? Or am I quietly working toward personal growth in a *fervent* manner?

The two are not the same.

Fer*vid* is defined as "impassioned, hot, boiling, extremely intense, nerved up, stressful, straining, or as the children say, beavering too eagerly.

Fer*vent* is defined as "enthusiastic, ardent, earnest, showing great warmth of feeling," but without any sense of stress or strain.

Each of them is an *attitude*.

You see each of them in operation all around you in modern America. For the past few decades our country has tended more toward the fervid pattern—good people straining so hard for "efficiency" in terms of money-making, while neglecting the truly fine art of successful living. You well know those types. They have firmly set lips, with chins thrust out, muscles taut, defiant glints in their eyes, making capitalistic competitiveness a horror. It is this that has created our unprecedented materialism; a worship of possessions, a feeling that ownership of "tangibles" is more important than thoughts, that status is more important than spirit.

This was not done intentionally; not really. We just sort of drifted into it, because of a burgeoning prosperity. But it soon became the most mistaken attitude in American history, resulting in that untenable outrage called tenure with its proliferating "government" (really a form of thievery) and its companion dragon known as inflation.

The good news, as this is written, is that the majority of us now realize our error, and are trying to correct it. One great national home-service magazine, with 8,000,000 circulation, polled 50,000 of its readers, asking "What do you consider the worst aspect of family life in America?" The answer ran about 90 percent, blaming "materialism," above spiritual values. And blaming *that* on fervid, competitive living.

So, there has been a recent reversal in the trend. Youngish married couples, with children especially, are reassessing their values and attitudes. They are less and less inclined to strain at impressing other people, or even themselves, with their prosperity and importance. A voter rebellion has arisen against outrageous taxation and foolish "government." In short, common sense may soon end our inflationary spiral and get us back to basics in our attitudes.

Again, dearly beloveds, I ask you—is the point clear?

Here at middle age or older, do you still feel that you must mortgage your soul in order to own an elaborate dwelling, a costly automobile or two, fancy motorcycles and sauna baths and liquor bars and showy clothing and gourmet foods and a boat in the harbor and a cottage on the lake and a lot of jewelry; and a lot of debt? Is your living fervent? Or fervid?

At your age, you are supposed to be intelligent!

Are you?

4

What You Say
And How You Say It

In the overall process of "adapting" to advancing age and upgrading the second half of our lives, we have to consider what personality blemishes, what "faults" we have allowed in ourselves.

Wherefore—what would you list as your worst fault? And my worst fault?

Extensive studies have been made into this. The answer was found, and verified. Most of your quick *guesses* would be wrong. Even when we are given the correct answer, we aging folk tend to glare for a few moments in indignation, even rejection and downright contempt. But on calm self-study, comes realization, understanding—and humble agreement. Then the climate is right for improvement.

Your worst fault, my worst fault, humanity's worst fault— undoubtedly is *imprecise communication in speech*. So say the experts.

Therefore the most important aspect of our lives is

what we say

and

how we say it.

I have indented for emphasis. The truth of that statement can never be too strongly emphasized. It was equally true when you were young, even in your childhood. But you were too unintelligent to realize it or admit it then. You lacked the control to benefit from the knowledge.

Here in your maturity, though, you *do* have capacity to

practice and vastly improve your speech. As a mature lady or gentleman mellowed by years of experience, you can *now* develop prompt control.

You can recognize that faulty communication is the basis of virtually all of mankind's mental miseries. This includes that horror of horrors, that experience so devastating to all concerned—the family quarrel.

It includes divorces, child delinquencies, business woes, faulty politics, even wars. We human beings—God's children, mind you—*simply do not communicate our true feelings to one another.*

We say the wrong words, in the wrong way.

"Wrong" as used here does not necessarily mean immoral or sinful or ungrammatical. Rather does it mean awkward, unfit, unreasonable, foolish, clumsy, careless, absurd, inept. The tone of voice itself is a major factor; tonal quality can generate deep emotions, malevolent or benign. "When you call me that—smile!" said the famous character in fiction. "Smiles," tenderness, good will—or lack of it—are more effectively projected by tone of voice than by choice of words. How you say it, can be infinitely more important than what you say.

IS YOUR REACTION NEGATIVE?

If you react negatively to the above summation, the chances are that it applies to you in full force. Your inherent conceit will not let you see the truth.

Many hundreds of thousands of men and women past age 40 are like that, the sociologists well know. Those multitudes have gradually established a set pattern or manner of speech, and it rarely ever occurs to them that it is faulty. "The person who is most self-centered," says one authority, a renowned psychiatrist,, "is paradoxically the least aware of it. And his associates are too hesitant or too awkward to point it out to him." Thus we struggle through life on verbal crutches.

Such dour citizens seem to fall into two main categories:

1. The financial and social "failures."

These can be very poor indeed, often living off kinsmen or on government dole. Many are resentful, without really knowing why. A few are simpleminded, even stupid. Most are sullen, defiant, selfish, and wallow in self-pity.

2. The well-to-do folk, who "have money" and mistakenly equate that with life success.

Arrogance is the hallmark of this group. They flush easily in anger. They want and demand their own way. They are "short" with humble clerks, waiters, waitresses, workers anywhere. They are introverted and self-pampering. The added tragedy is that they usually are otherwise very intelligent, heart-hungry people. Somehow, they have simply missed the boat.

BUT MANY ARE RADIANT

Offsetting those two dour types are what we call the radiant people—and I admonish you to study them carefully and join their clan, if you are not already among them.

Somehow these aging women and men do indeed just seem to *radiate* cheerfulness, contentment, inner happiness, good will. There is no hint of pose or put-on about it. You just sense that such is their life way. Quite naturally, they are the best loved people on earth, because they themselves dispense love.

As a for-instance I think of M.J. and Eugenia Pipsaire. That is an old Louisiana-French name of distinction, in this case for a very handsome, tall, smiling, curly-haired, sharp-minded, aging executive in a big savings and loan association. He started courting pretty Eugenia Preston away back yonder in the Dark Ages when people had—you know—touring cars: Two-seaters, with tops that would fold down? M.J., a sterling teenager, came to her small town and she spotted him. How to get acquainted? Well youth is youth, so she conned her brother Billy into driving alongside another open car in which the handsome newcomer sat, and she threw a big gooey red heart of a watermelon into the young Pipsaire face.

Never mind, now, all the repercussions; just remember

that courtship is a variant. Today those two have been happily married for a long, long time, and it is the good fortune of my Adele and me to be close friends to them, so that we know the way they operate, we see their attitudes and hear the way they talk.

"HEY!" both always shout, running out to meet us when we call. "How great it is to see you! You are both looking wonderful." (We are much older than they). "Come on in here!" A pause to hug and kiss us, take our coats, *glow* at us. It is all genuine, there is no over-effusiveness, no false front. We feel their goodness because *they* feel it and show it. "Come in here and we will have some tea before suppertime. The young turnip greens in my flower bed are just tender and right for boiling how are your daughters and your grandchildren what all have you folks been doing and can you stay with us for—"M.J. interrupted there, I recall, grabbing my shoulders and shaking me and grinning as he too rattled on "—we'll cook them with hog fat and have hot cornbread and peach cobbler and you are retired now and we have this big new mobile home it sleeps six and you two will go to Canada with us we'll see Banff and maybe go on into Alaska—" Eugenia again. "—of *course* you can go with us we want you we will have a reception here for you tomorrow night then next day we will go fishing on the lake the trout are rising wonderfully this week and I know that you—"

It was a cascade. A flow tide of love and wonder and goodness. It happened precisely that way a short time ago. An outpouring, an eagerness, every time we go there. They do not talk of themselves, they show exhuberant concern for *us*. They want to share their blessings.

Are *you* like that, dearly beloveds who read here? I hope you are. This is a book to help you upgrade the remainder of your life, you know. Take heed!

Enthusiasm always is contagious. You can have enthusiasm for zestful living no matter what your age—and *selfless loving communication is the best part of it*. It reaches the zenith of grandeur when used between man and wife, or by the two of them facing kin and friends. Of all the most wonderful, magical and powerful tools in the world, nice words rank first.

No, it is not imperative that you speak heartily and exhuberantly like that. Eugenia's brother, president of that same big savings and loan association, is much more reserved, as is his Nancy. When we went to their house, though, their eyes lit up, their faces were beaming. The voices were softer, but the hugs were tight. "You must stay at least a month," Nancy ordered. "Two months," Billy endorsed. "You are retired. Our boys are grown up and gone, we have those two big rooms upstairs, we have a wonderful hired cook, we will drive you to Houston and San Antonio, we will—"

"Shut up," I had to say. "I came to play you some golf and go fishing with you. How are you doin', old coots?"

He ignored me. "You can have your mail forwarded here. The four of us will go to Vermont in October and see the glorious autumn colors." (Incidentally, we did just that.) Nancy picked it up, "We will have little granddaughter Sarah here with her parents for dinner with you. Tomorrow we will—" On and on, and on. Communication. *Love* communication, selfless communication. Joy of living. Pure and kind hearts.

EVERY MORNING AT 11 O'CLOCK

Another magnificent for-instance, which I have detailed in my book titled *A Boundless Privilege* (published by University of Texas Press under its trade imprint, Madrona Press, Austin, Texas).

In 1908 Opal was the prettiest teenager in her state—I quote all who knew her, and I agree. Her small town swains flitted around her like moths. But comes to town a city dude named Ned, a nice fellow who made a success in insurance. He discovered Opal, proposed, and married her in her home at exactly 11 o'clock one morning.

Now get this:

Literally every day for the rest of his 52 years of marriage to

Opal, *he either called at home or telephoned her at exactly 11 o'clock in the morning!*

Every day!

If he had a valued customer in his office, or if he was in a very important meeting of his Board of Directors—a pause while he telephoned the wife he called "Doll." If he had to be in New York City or Chicago, he did that. At precisely 11:00 a.m. Love talk, for five expensive minutes across a continent. "Communication" at its peak of perfection, day in and day out. Ned died an honored and happy man; Opal followed him within a few years. She too had loved, not only her Ned but seemingly every human being on earth. I know whereof I speak; she was my sister.

Once again—is my point clear? I feel sure that it is.

I could list dozens of examples, showing people happy in successful family living and community affairs because they *do* habitually say the right thing in the right way. The importance of this is beyond measuring.

You'd think that our schools would all teach young people this profound truth and technique. They do not. Many schools seem too confounded "academic"—whatever that means—to realize that simple communication is paramount. Even half or more of our teachers today are incompetents in getting their knowledge across. They cannot teach children, or even young adults in college, to choose words carefully so as to convey exact meanings, and to enunciate clearly, and to LISTEN courteously with concentration. We spend millions on gymnasiums and football teams and science laboratories but neglect this basic, all-important need in our schools.

The same lamentations apply in our writing. Strangely, the simple act of writing a letter to a mother or wife or husband or any other person, becomes an almost insurmountable roadblock for millions of men and women who consider themselves educated and intelligent. In stupid self-pity we exclaim "Oh I don't like to write letters, I can't write good ones." Stupid indeed! *Of course* you can write good letters, if you can read and write at all.

The same basic outreach in writing applies as it does in speech—common sense. When you write, *consider the reader*. A letter of complaint, a letter giving a lot of unwanted free advice? Never! Many people seem to think that any letter must be rather formal, that it must follow exact precedent, must be a work of literature, grammatically perfect. Nonsense! You don't even need to start your letter with "Dear" So-and-so, especially a business letter. I start most of mine by saying "Greetings to (NAME)." Simple greetings. Often I just say, "Hi, there!" for my opener. Then I go on in friendly informal tone. I try to show an interest in the reader and his/her affairs.

LEARN TO *LISTEN*

Even worse than our failure to speak effectively, is our sad unwillingness to LISTEN attentively. This seems true of virtually everybody in some degree, but it tends to get worse as we age along. Now that we have aged up close to 40 or more, we assume that we have all the answers to life's problems, hence are obligated to talk rather than listen. Phooey! Correct that by looking your companion straight in the eye—and remaining quiet. When he/she has finished, add whatever might be *relevant and encouraging*, then let the other person continue. I guarantee you will learn more, and will soon have a reputation for being a superb conversationalist. There are some exceptions; occasionally you encounter a compulsive "talker" who just rattles on unbearably. Clip that one off, and put distance between you. In truth, though, most compulsive talkers are pitifully lonely people, so very anxious to have rapport with some fellow human beings. Often, therefore, I just sit or stand and listen, even to them. But I listen only with what I call the top of my mind; the bottom part may be wandering into more interesting fields.

Middle age—I repeat—is the best time to upgrade your speaking and listening abilities. Do not wait too long, or you will have become too deeply grooved in the bad habits. Then if you don't watch yourself, you will have degenerated into being one of those old gaffers or gals who talk incessantly and boringly about "the old days" of your youth. Some artful reminiscing is very fine indeed. But be wary! Be very sparing of it, be choosy.

Making the second half of your life the BEST part, positively does depend largely on how much you improve your communications; what you say, and how you say it.

DEVELOPING EXPERTISE

Reading *aloud* is a great help in this self-improvement reach for expertise. This offers a double reward: not only will you improve your voice by focusing on it and exercising it with care, but you just might learn some good things from what you read! If possible, read aloud into a tape recorder so that you can play it all back and study your own voice. This can be immensely helpful.

WHAT shall you read?

It doesn't matter too much; whatever is in good taste, whatever interests you and seems clean and rewarding. I recommend at least some poetry.

Too few people read poetry. Old men especially tend to sneer at it, calling it impractical, childish, silly. They are thereby advertising their own mental and emotional ignorance. Truth is, good poetry is more wonderful than good prose. Much of the Holy Bible is in poetry—did you realize that? Come to think on it—what IS poetry? How is it defined?

The best definition says that "Poetry is thought—*felt*."

No, it does not have to rhyme; it is never imperative to say that "Roses are red and violets are blue, Sugar is sweet and I love you." That's okay for third grade in elementary school, but not for you folk who are past age 30 and "getting along." Nor do you have to be as vaguely literary as, let us say, Mister William Shakespeare, or that silly old poetess who said "A rose is a rose is a rose" and parlayed that into fame.

Fundamentally, poetry means that you, sir, do not say to

Minnie Smith, "Your eyes are blue." That is a mere bald, prosaic statement of biological fact. If you want Minnie to smile on you and invite you to dinner and maybe marry up with you later, you must say to her, "Miss Minerva, your eyes are my windows of paradise."

You think I'm joking?

I'm not! In each of those statements you have said the same thing, basically, but in the second statement you were poetic with it—understand? Your thoughts about Minnie, was *felt!* And in that second expression of it, she got the message, you can be sure. You were not a clod; you were a sensitive man of imagination and charm.

In choosing your poetry for reading, aloud or otherwise, you do need to be discriminating. For example, I am forced to tell you, my aging friend, that Mr. Edgar Guest was not, is not, the world's greatest poet. Frankly, I don't know WHO is.

But I can assure you that poetry is close akin to music, and that in listening to and studying each of those great forms of communication, you can make rapid progress upward, indeed you can soon rise to the heights. It is nice and sweet to sing with the little Sunday School children that "Je-suss luffs me, this I know, Because The Bi-bell tells me so." That's poetry, of a sort; that's music, of a sort. But it is quite another thing to stand up in church and roar out "HALLE-LUJAH! . . . HALLELUJAH! . . . HALLELUJAH! . . . HAL-LELUJAH!" with the great chancel choir and organ on Easter morn. Just one word of praise, repeated. Yet Mr. Handel knew what he was doing; he knew well that he was touching our hearts not only with music but with poetry, because poetry is *thought—felt.* No wonder that Hallelujah Chorus ranks as the grandest of all musical compositions.

FELICITY

Any earnest study of poetry simply helps you develop what we authors call felicity of expression; which is to say, expertise in human communication. As you read good poetry, you are sure to become "hooked" on it after a few trials. You will be going around muttering something about "the tintinnabulation of the bells, the bells bells, bells bells, bells bells bells." True, that may cause your friends to lift finger to their heads, look wide-eyed at other people, make a circle with that finger, then be extra kind to you. But so what? Grin at them; and tell the clunks that Mister Edgar Allen Poe was a genius at human communication. Hang in there, Buster and Bertha, and run your own life, you and you alone can upgrade it.

THE COMPLIMENT CLUB!

Finally, in upgrading the New You, in enriching your final years on earth beginning right now, for heaven's sake do learn the communicative art of paying a compliment. Doing this alone can become, literally, The Best Part of Your Life.

How very hard it is—how very *rare* it is—for most of us to pay a verbal compliment, expressing heartfelt appreciation! This, even though all psychologists and other authorities (not to mention common sense and experience) tell us that the need and craving for recognition and approval are paramount in every human being.

Literally, we live for approval.

We live for the approval of others, even though we may not realize it, may in fact deny it. Not *giving* that recognition, or denying our interest in receiving it, is probably the most devastating failure in our routine living. It is important enough that George W. Crane, M.D., Ph.D., America's foremost practical psychologist and author in this field, has launched a national non-profit "Compliment Club" to help us negligent average citizens. As mentioned earlier, I have spent long hours, days, nights, with Dr. Crane, have seen his mail arrive not in bags but in truck loads. I well know that he touched a national humanitarian nerve.

Strangest part of it all is—giving someone recognition and deserved praise, is a totally *pleasant* process, a mutually happy thing to do in our daily communications. Therefore, WHY are we so reluctant?

There is no logical answer. We retreat by saying "It is just human nature" to be reticent and take other persons' achievements for granted. Well, nuts to "human nature," then; that phase of it is ultra-stupid. *Human nature is individual, and is what each human being makes it, and is subject to change.* That fact is indeed the very premise of this book. If "human nature" couldn't be changed readily by each individual, there could never be any form of personal growth or advancement; all of us would still be cave women or men.

TWO AREAS FOR USING PRAISE

There are two major areas in which we intelligent folk neglect the powerful truths about appreciation:

1. In business life, including schools.

The boss, the supervisor, the teacher, the foreman, demands much of his charges. It is right that he or she should do precisely that. The worker is paid, hence is obligated to do his very best. This is a standard dictum around the world and always has been; the worker is worthy of his hire if—and only if—he gives his best effort. (Teachers are both workers and bosses.)

But all of that is mere survival motivation. It can actually become competitive, within its own framework; resentments can interfere. So what about a *higher*, more inspiriting encouragement?

Indeed there does have to be a "human" factor, something to do with the human psyche, the inner being; an inspiration, a soul exaltation far more powerful than a pay envelope. When and only when this is present is the laborer's production happily doubled, tripled, seemingly with no more effort at all. Whereupon "the boss" profits more in proportion.

That bonus for both sides comes only when cordial,

sincere appreciation is expressed; that is to say, when a compliment is paid.

Monetary expression (increase in wages) is not enough. The worker positively needs to be recognized, honored. This need not be gushy, and does not have to be given for every trivial achievement; it must not be transparent, because any adult will sense insincerity at once. Similarly, the lofty boss himself craves approval, so that an occasional thank-you from his workers is called for. No, you dare not "butter up" the boss; he will fire you for that, and well he should. But if he is doing a good job of bossing—tell him (or maybe it's a her) that you recognize it and appreciate it. This can work magic in both your lives.

2. In the home.

It should be unnecessary to blueprint this matter for your use in the home. You are intelligent (only people with intelligence read my books!). So you realize that the Compliment Club psychologies outlined above must in fact begin in the home. In fact it must begin before you even establish the new home; you must "say nice things," meaningfully, earnestly, feelingly, to the person you hope to marry. Then surely, surely, you must say them to your mate.

"You look radiant this morning!" I may say to my Adele, when she comes from our bedroom to cook my breakfast.

That not only gets me a good breakfast, it gets me a kiss and a happy day's launching. Malarky? Of course it is—I am an Irishman. But it is *genuine* malarky. I mean it. She *does* come in glowing; her costume neat, her hair combed, her face smiling. I love the old gal, so I grab her and hug her and start preparing the grapefruit for us and maybe whap her once on the rump in passing and she is likely to be humming and saying she won't need the car today I can have it to go play golf and you must feel good, the way you are grinning this morning. I *do* feel good. I appreciate my wife and tell her so, and I get appreciated in turn. Is my point here clear, dearly beloveds?

The children, now.

Oh good heavens, if I have to tell you that your children all need and crave approval from their parents, you had best resign from the human race.

Discipline? Nuts to discipline. The stern father is an abomination on earth, the tight-lipped no-nonsense mother is a female jerk. Neither is fit to be a parent.

Yes, yes, I know—you have to be in charge. You do indeed have to set standards—reasonable ones—and see that the offspring live up to them. But I swear to you that encouragement and good-natured rapport is ten thousand times as effective in rearing children as are hard-boiled "rules and regulations," threats and whippings and other punishments. A current bumper sticker asks, "HAVE YOU HUGGED YOUR CHILD TODAY?" Well, have you?

If you can't understand what I'm saying here, please put all your children up for adoption. You do not deserve them, and some more deeply spiritual foster parents can rear them into topflight, happy citizens.

5

You Are Too Sharp
To Be So Dull

The foregoing chapter leads us quickly to consideration of an attitude which too few of us ever take seriously, because it seemingly has nothing to do with seriousness, indeed at first it appears almost too trivial for any attention at all.

In point of fact, it is extremely important: *especially* for people middle-aged and older, who tend to become grooved in habits of dour thinking, speech and action. It is best stated as follows:

If you are going to make the second half the best part of your life, *you positively do need a lot of fun in it*. Fun! Humor! Laughter!

That is no "joking" matter. Harken to the way it is expressed by one distinguished authority, Robert Wells Youngs, D.D., senior pastor of a big church in Pompano Beach, Florida, and author of *What It Means To Be A Christian*, which I rate as the most inspired, helpful and enjoyable book I have ever read outside of the Bible itself. He also has a fine book of short devotionals titled *Renewing Your Faith Day By Day* (Doubleday) and in that he says—

"How much easier it is to live with ourselves and others if we have a cheerful disposition and especially a sense of humor. One thinks of Socrates on that day when his wife scolded him with scornful words and then dumped a bucket of water over his head. Did Socrates react as most men would have done? No. Being a true philosopher, he remarked that after so much thunder and lightening, he expected a shower. Humor takes the tension out of angry situations. It is a saving grace in all human relationships."

So there you have it from two truly high-level authorities, one current and one immortal because of the wisdom he left us many centuries ago. Virtually every other modern authority agrees with them; the sociologists, psychiatrists, psychologists, clergymen. So does the Holy Bible. In Proverbs it says, "Pleasant words are as a honeycomb, sweet to the soul, and health to the bones."

ABOUT YOURSELF, NOW

So how about yourself, sir and madam, here in the late 20th century A.D., you who are "getting along" in years and drifting into dullness? It is time for a multiphasic personality inventory!

Let us begin it with a study of the five old gents, very old, who were settin' make that sitting on a park bench. Two beautiful shapely young maidens walked by. Presently one of the old gaffers croaked, "Can you fellers remember when we used to kiss girls?"

The others nodded. They did remember. Then in weak, wistful, tremolo voice, one of them asked, "Wasn't there something else?"

Whenever I tell that yarn, which is often, I always get a fine character and personality study. Ninety percent or so of the men and women in my audience burst out in laughter. The others tend to smile weakly if at all, and some frown in obvious disapproval.

What was *your* reaction?

It is a good test story, because the response it evokes can be very revealing. It is not offensive, even though there is a tiny innuendo. So if you took umbrage there, if your reaction was negative, you probably belong to the most pitiable of all people—those without a wholesome healthy *sense of humor*.

There is also another little fun gimmick that I use in lectures and parlor conversations. (Parlor? Who ever has a "parlor" nowadays? That dates me! But you know what I mean). I ask my listeners if they know what the word *genetics* means. (Incidentally, do you?)

Most educated folk have heard of it, naturally; yet very few of them are quite sure that they understand it fully. A lady in one recent audience, very alert, eyes sparkling, replied, "I think it refers to ingredients that make up a pizza."

Not bad! She had lightened the atmosphere; we were on our way to a delightful evening. Pizza is indeed an Italian mishmash of materials into which anything goes, and genetics seems to be something like that. Not bad at all, that crack!

But I had to hold center stage—natch—so I enlightened the 100 or so folk on this occasion by telling them that "The first law of genetics says that *if your parents never had any children, the chances are you won't have any either.*"

Now there was a good sound piece of serious scientific deduction. But sweet Melissa Wimbish, aged 53, did not quite understand it. No whit timid, she spoke out—"But see here, if your parents never had any children, how could *you* be here yourself?"

I love Melissa. She is my elder daughter's close friend. But the sweet lady is so literal minded that it is painful for a zany Irishman to fraternize with her. Somebody had to spell it all out for Lissa, and when it finally did come through to her, she smiled and laughed gaily, alone. While the other folk surreptitiously smiled at her.

ABOUT YOURSELF, AGAIN

Now about you again, madam or sir: *If you felt any negative reaction to the above bits of humor, you are in trouble.*

Your age in this instance has nought to do with it. Even a normal 12-year-old would have responded properly, as would a normal 90-year-old. The two little jokes are harmless. In fact they are rather cute and clever and entertaining (I did not originate them, and I don't know who did). But if you feel slightly disdainful of them or consider them too trivial for consideration, then a very, very important part of your personality has not been developed. You are a dull person, probably without realizing what a wonderful lifelong

happiness you have missed. Because the gospel truth is—
   A wholesome sense of humor is as important to
   successful living as is a wholesome sense of morals.

That statement is not merely something off the top of my so-called mind, it is a positive clinical fact, stressed by all those authorities I mentioned, especially the clergymen and rabbis and psychologists. Not to mention common sense.

If you are morally "good," but have not a sense of humor, you are only half a woman or man.

Being moral, Christian, or god-fearing in any religion, is not enough. If you adhere to the teachings of your minister, priest or rabbi, your guru or whoever your leader may be, if you religiously read the Bible, Talmud, Koran and other sacred literature, if you pray devoutly every dawn and dusk, if you live circumspectly 24 hours every day—and have not a sense of humor—your personality is still only at half-way point.

But there are millions like you. Especially does many a present-day aging person—say 40 to 70—nurse an emotional heritage from the Puritanical Victorian era. These folk tend to be rigid in morals, but defiant against laughter and fun.

THE BALANCING FORCE

Your sense of humor balances your sense of morals.

If you are *just* moral, you are likely to be overly pious and authoritarian. You develop a habit of self-righteously judging other people's morals—when in truth such judging is strictly a prerogative of God. You become emotionally and religiously stern. You have a set face; and a set mind. You decry all "foolishness," and are disdainful of those who seem to court it and dish it out.

More accurately, that is the way you *appear* to be.

Secretly, most of you literal-minded and non-humorous folk are really envious. You see the rest of us engaged in high-jenks *joie de vivre—joy of living*—you hear us laugh and fraternize and swap small talk and sing together and walk together hand in hand swinging our hands with our faces to the sky. And you feel left out, forlorn. Tragically, you ask yourself, what do these people have that I lack? Tragically!

"Humor," says the great psychiatrist, William Bede McGrath, M.D., author of the book *Mental Fitness*, "is the calisthenics of the mind."

He also says that most of his worst mental cases among people of all ages, but especially among those at 40 or more, seem to have no sense of humor whatsoever, no fun in life at all.

In a sense, the Pilgrim Fathers are to blame for this in America. The Puritans. Perhaps we can excuse them for it. *Their* problem, almost insurmountable, was sheer survival; fighting off hostile Indians, working like dogs eking out a living from soil and forest. They had no doctors, no hospitals, no corner drugstore to supply them with aspirin, Valium or other tranquilizers. They actually had no telephones, no television, no citizen band radios! Those poor dears. Stark living!

But centuries have passed. And we moderns *do* have time and opportunity for fun. And *do* realize the importance of it. So if you are a humorless person—why?

SECOND ONLY TO CREATIVITY

All authorities agree that humor is not only the calisthenics which tone your emotional muscles, it is second only to creativity in guaranteeing happiness in old age. In point of fact, humor itself is creative; the two concepts go hand in hand.

This does not require you to become a stand-up or even a sit-down comedian. Please, please, do not try to be a Bob Hope! That most famous of modern comics is unique, but if you strain to emulate him you will likely end up making a fool of yourself. Anyway, his output is not at all what is meant when those authorities refer to a sense of humor.

Note carefully:

The term "sense of humor" does *not* mean merely the habitual cracking of jokes. It does *not* require skill at badinage and persiflage and clever repartee in the cocktail lounge.

It refers, rather, to your habitual *reactions* to life-routine phenomena of almost all kinds.

It suggests that all of us have to "laugh it off" when something unwelcome happens beyond our control. No, not death or disaster; but in the events of ordinary home and business relations.

You must learn *not* to "take umbrage"— an old-fashioned term which I throw around, in wry fun. You must react with quiet good humor whenever your wife or your husband "sasses" you or speaks in terse "short" tone. Unkind words from a mate or a child nearly always stem from physical or emotional fatigue; they are not really meant to be ugly or spiteful or vindictive or mean, they are simply inept communication, due to the stress of the moment. Can you grasp that very important truism? The self-controlled individual never allows another's mood to distress him or her. Snappishness, moodiness, fatigue, are the basis of most petty bickerings that are observed between aging couples.

Can you learn to "skip it"?

Not "make something of it"?

Not feel touchy, defiant, eager for spiteful comeback or a put-down thrust of revenge? The anatomy of anger is a profound one. Even such factors as a woman's menstrual periods can critically affect her anger cycle. Any man's sex life, or lack of it, is a major factor. Business disappointments, social failures or neglect, loneliness, all play their parts. But knowing this, you can be prepared, you can outwit such influences.

In short, you are an intelligent person, so you need only to take charge of yourself, and recognize that you are much too sharp to be so dull.

SUPPLEMENT FOR SHARPNESS

Many earnest aging folk begin to take life seriously because they simply do not know any "funny stories" to tell.

They yearn to be happy-humored but have lost the knack of it, hence they retreat from the more abundant life into moribundant living routine.

In my files (due to years of compiling books of humor) are at least 100,000 jokes and "stories," some apocraphal, many taken from real life. There are two main sources of spontaneous humor: the home and the church. Best of all probably is the humor of innocence.

As, for instance, the matchless saga of little uninhibited Snitchacookie Jones. That 5-year-old twerp came into the church patio for fellowship hour, after Sunday worship inside with his mama. He stopped before a grossly fat and unornamental woman, gazed up at her and said, "Gol-lee, you sure are ugly."

Naturally, his mama was appalled. She jerked the lad off to one side, shook him firmly and said, "Shame on you, sonny! You have hurt that nice old lady's feelings. Now you just go right back over there and tell her you are sorry."

So all right, he obeyed his Mom. He paddled over to the fat lady again, turned his big serious eyes up at her and said distinctly so that several people heard him—"I am SORRY you are ugly!"

* * *

And how about the little sweetie-pie girl who, along with 30 or so of her companions, had been gathered down front in the church sanctuary, on the altar steps, to hear pretty young matron Mrs. Pat Drew give them a quickie sermonette in the Democratic year of 1978? She told the children about important men in the Bible; mentioned Adam, Moses, Joseph, Paul and of course Jesus. Then she tested them asking, "Now who is the very MOST important man in the Bible?"

Come to think on it, how would you answer that? Pat Drew figured that the answer would be Jesus. But after a moment of silence, with all of us in the church listening, little Linda Malloy shouted out—"JIMMIE CARTER?"

* * *

Consider now the hypothetical town of Palm Springs, Alaska. There dwelt the good Reverend Doctor Saddlie Thredbaire, underpaid pastor of the Gesundt Heights Baptist Church. For 40 years he had worked hard without a vacation. Suddenly a rich parishioner—who had made a financial killing on the great pipeline—financed the old pastor for a month's vacation trip.

Thus Dr. Thredbaire went south to Arizona, in what Alaskans call "the lower 48." He got to a dude ranch, located smack on top of that state's famous Tonto Rim. Exceedingly picturesque, and dangerous, that Rim is about 100 miles long, an upthrust of rock cliff 2,000 feet into the sky.

The dude ranch corral was about 100 yards from that sheer drop-off 2,000 feet straight down. After breakfast on his first morning at the ranch, Dr. Thredbaire walked happily out to the corral and said to the head wrangler, "I love being in the Wild West, but I have never ridden a horse. Do you happen to have any horses that an old preacher might ride?"

The courteous wrangler smiled and replied, "Why yes sir, we sure do. In fact we have one trained especially for clergymen. This horse does not understand the usual commands, like 'Giddap' and 'Whoa.' If you want him to leap forward instantly and gallop fast, just say to him 'PRAISE THE LORD.' If you want him to stop instantly, say 'AMEN.' "

"That's the one for me!" exclaimed the happy old preacher.

So they helped him into the saddle. He took the bridle reins, patted the horse's neck, and said "Giddap."

Nothing happened; the horse did not move. Then the wrangler whispered a reminder.

"Oh, of course," the preacher smiled benignly. "Sorry. PRAISE THE LORD!"

Instantly the horse leaped out as if jet-propelled. Went clat-a-clat bookety-bookety with head down—straight toward that Tonto Rim drop-off yonder just 100 yards away. He would soon plunge over. Realizing the danger, Dr. Threadbaire panicked and shouted, "WHOA, WHOA!"

The stupid horse plunged on, head down, unseeing.

Dr. Thredbaire's panic quadrupled. Death was eminent; they would surely plunge over that 2,000-foot cliff onto jagged rocks below.

But lo—in the split-second nick of time, he remembered. He shouted "AMEN!" And yes sir, the horse skidded to a stop, with its very nose hanging over that Rim. The good preacher's life was saved.

He was so grateful, that he looked up to heaven and in gratitude shouted "PRAISE THE LORD!"

*   *   *

This one is a classic. A noted medium, Miss Clair Voyant, had staged a dinner party back yonder in 1910 honoring a certain Mr. Samuel L. Clemens, of whom you will have heard.

Table talk got around to the matter of punishment in the hereafter. Many opinions were aired, as to which of their deceased friends had gone to heaven and which to hell. Finally Miss Voyant turned to the guest of honor and asked Mr. Twain for his opinion.

"You will have to excuse me," replied that famous wit. "I remain silent from necessity, because I have many friends in both places."

*   *   *

Old man Vernon Vicissitude was fed up with all this—you know—modernity and such like. "If the safety pin had been invented here in 1979," he groused, "it would have seven transistors, a rheostat, nine moving parts, and require a service man four times a year."

*   *   *

That renowned physician Dr. Bill Zarhigh arrived late for an operation at the hospital one recent morning. He grimly apologized to his patient by saying, "A bulldog hanging onto something is not the ultimate in tenacity. It cannot compare with a stuck zipper."

* * *

"I am a man without an enemy in this world," declared 99-year-old Mort Gage, the former bank president. "I have outlived all of them."

To which his pal Clarion Call, the former newspaper publisher, replied. "I am younger than you, but I too am a man without a single enemy."

"How can you say that?" Mort demanded.

"Because they are all married."

* * *

Mr. Fuseloyle Gaspayne, aged 67, was in the office of his physician when an extremely attractive young nurse walked through.

"Holy Moses!" the old gent murmured, eyes wide. "Now that is a mighty pretty young girl."

"Seven kids," the doctor replied laconically. "All grown and married."

"Oh come on!" Fuseloyle protested. "*She* doesn't have seven grown children."

"No," admitted the doctor. "But you do."

* * *

Any man is just as old as he feels. But when he is as old as you are sir, and starts feeling, he gets slapped.

* * *

And now in conclusion, gentlemen—whenever you feel yourself burning with desire to do something worthwhile, just be careful you don't make an ash of yourself.

6

Make No Plans
For "Retirement"

At ages 36 to 40 or so men and women begin to make their first feeble jokes about aging.

Prior to that, we are never going to *be* old; if the thought enters our consciousness at all it is promptly pushed back out. We still have sexual virility, we still charge boldly up to the net in tennis for a magnificent kill, we drive our cars with perfect automatic reaction timing, we work hard and accomplish things, we "run the tower" (or so we think)—and we laugh, not always politely, at the "old folk."

Then on the morning after the 40th birthday party—ah ha!

Suddenly the future is here now. "Some day," for getting old, is just yonder on the near horizon.

This syndrome is always depressing. Many people, especially women, panic when they abruptly realize that they are getting old. With horror they perceive crows' feet near the eyes, wiggly worm tracks on the neck, a down tilt of the mouth. Old Age! "Dreams are for sale?" No! Only Realities now exist, and the future is bleak. Many a million has shed bitter tears at this breakpoint in life.

And then plunged right into a welter of self-pity, which is an excellent prelude to that horrible old-age state called senility.

THE COLD TRUTH

The cold truth of the matter, however, is that dreams *are* still for sale. The best dreams ever. Because these are not the vaporous, romantic yearnings of immaturity and youth, these are dreams that can indeed be realized, be given substance. But the good ones come high in price; they require some hard thinking and praying and effort if they are to come true.

The first recommended step is to re-explore that inevitability in your life called aging.

Scientists now know that it is unnecessary! Aging is primarily a matter of chemistry. Give our experts a few more years and—brother! People will be living to ages 100, 120, 150, in normal routine, and in excellent health both physically and mentally. This is one of the Grand Dreams, now coming true.

Consider your physical body right this moment. *It is not the same physical body that housed you four months ago!* Every cell in every human body of every age, is replaced once in 120 days. (One main authority for that startling statement is Dr. Marvel Bessis, professor of the famed Institute of Cellular Pathology in Paris.)

I would never have guessed that. I look at my hand. Surely it is the same hand that I used to light the Christmas table candles nine months ago? Isn't it? It has to be!

It isn't. It is only the *form* of that same hand. Those cells that held the match last Christmas are long sluffed off, wasted away and departed. New ones have come in twice since then, and will continue to change in a moment-by-moment process until we die.

That scientific truth disturbs me considerably. On the other hand, it also stimulates me considerably, just as it is stimulating the minds of the experts in cellular pathology. "Newness," then, is physical with each of us individually, and always has been. What is *really* new is the fact that those experts are rapidly learning ways to control and extend the renewing process, learning ways to delay bodily deterioration.

As a result, we the-people-of-the-pasture may confidently expect lives of 200 years or longer by the middle Century 21. This generates exhilarating thoughts on behalf of our present grandchildren.

SENILITY IS UNNECESSARY

Best new fact about all that is—you and I, in our physical time here, can now hope to avoid that horrifying state called senility.

Awareness of that malady usually strikes suddenly. One day we visit our beloved older friends Jonathan and Mary Doe, and we come home deeply depressed. Because, to our utter consternation and despair, poor John has become senile.

Senile!

My friend John (or my friend Mary).

Hadn't seen him since he moved to his daughter's town over a year ago—and when I got there he didn't know me. Impossible! Why, we grew up together. We worked in the same office. We played golf every Saturday. He worked hard in our church, he was a fine, intelligent man in every way.

Now his memory seems gone, his eyes are glazed, his mouth hangs open, he acts "lost" and even has to be helped to dress and undress. His wife Mary cried, privately, talking with my wife. I feel like crying myself.

The case history is not unique. There are thousands of "senior citizens" who are little more than walking vegetables.

HARDENING OF THE ARTERIES: . . . NO!

So then we fortunate ones are suddenly more than sympathetic, we are alarmed. We are afraid for ourselves. Being sensible, we therefore look into the matter at once.

Right off, somebody tells us that poor John's condition is due to hardening of the arteries. The technical term for it is arteriosclerosis. That name sounds frightening, hence our fears are increased. Arteries harden, thereby cutting off the blood supply to the brain, which in turn makes poor John or any other aging person senile—right?

Wrong!

Largely wrong.

Oh yes, some doctors still insist; the old-hat ones. But it

took 50 years to make doctors stop "bleeding" people for every ailment under the sun; remember; took generations for them to understand that "laudable pus" which they encouraged in any wound was actually far from laudable, was in fact a sign of vicious infection likely to kill than cure the patient. Physicians are not sacrosanct. They are human beings who tend to become self-satisfied and authoritarian—even as you and I. They can be wrong, and frequently are.

But here in the last quarter of the Golden Century, intelligent open-minded young researchers have determined the *real* cause of senility and—better yet—have shown us how to prevent it.

Which may be the best news I can bring you in this book.

DO NOT BECOME A MENTAL OYSTER

Let us assume that you, an intelligent person well along in years, lay down in bed and stayed there, completely inactive for six to eight months.

You would become a physical oyster.

Now let us assume that you ceased all but the minimal routine of thinking, just "did nothing" mentally for six or eight months.

You would become a mental oyster.

From that hypothesis we can deduce something highly important for every person past age 40 to realize—

Senility is caused primarily
by *mental* retirement.

Manifestations of it can develop in men or women in the age 40s when they become affluent enough to cease working and begin pampering themselves. They establish a self-centered routine—and coast. Or as one authority expressed it, they stop thinking and start drinking. The drinking is primarily to stifle boredom with life.

So—

Keep your body exercised and fed sensibly, and you can virtually guarantee yourself good physical health.

Keep your *mind* exercised and fed sensibly, and you can

virtually guarantee yourself lasting mental health.

It is as simple as that.

It is an inspiring reality; an exciting new reassurance for every woman and man.

IMPORTANT BACKGROUND KNOWLEDGE

So that you can truly focus on this vital matter of avoiding mental retirement and senility, we must refresh our knowledge of historic American mores and manners, habit patterns in thinking. First, let me repeat—we should expunge the word "retirement" from the language.

Why, for heaven's sake, should anybody ever "retire" just to sit around and do nothing, in the old concept of that? If sickness or other informities force you to be inactive physically, nearly always there are still stimulating mental outlets for you.

"But I *deserve* retirement!" you may counter. "I have earned the right to stop work and let my children or somebody take care of me for the rest of my life."

No such. Old age is, by all standards, a do-it-yourself project. Literally, you must guide yourself through old age, you must continue to "paddle your own canoe" until the day you die if at all possible. Nobody "owes" you anything, except what you owe yourself.

From the employers' point of view—"retire" a good worker at age 65? Preposterous! Our school systems and banks and factories and other business institutions got trapped by the thought of mandatory retirement of employees at age 65 or thereabouts, and it is interesting folk history to learn why it happened.

Conceivably those businesses had a point when the pattern started away back yonder in the 19th century. In that era life expectancy was only about 48 to 50 years. America was largely an agrarian nation, and generally a farmer was "done" by age 40 or so. He was worn out, finished, tired, through, over the hill. Death beckoned. Indeed at that moment he often melodramatically carved out his own tombstone, laid elaborate plans for his funeral, then sat around waiting to die. And died.

That early death was due to several factors, such as poor diet and poor sanitation, due to limited knowledge of bodily needs, negligible knowledge of mental and spiritual potential. Modern folk today have no real appreciation of how *well* they eat, how scientific and clean their diets really are, compared to the diets of our ancestors. Man is an animal, and animals in general eat by hunger demand and are never too choosy and pay little attention to sanitation and chemical need. This controls the horses, cows, lions, tigers, birds, fishes and all other creatures, which with rare exception are short-lived.

But Man was made—divine? Put in charge? Told to use his brain and improve his status? Obviously so. He has done just that, so his life span has been increased. Present-day experts in this field say that by the year 2,000 life expectancy will certainly be well over 100 years, and close to 200 in mid-century. These experts are tightening down the cause of aging, and eliminating them. Whole new concepts of body chemistry have been developed and are still being expanded. This includes close study of the so-called trace minerals, many of which are known to have profound influence on our lives, and all of which are found in ocean water. Shall we, then, start drinking a little ocean water every day, just to be sure we get them, much as we now gulp vitamins? Some researchers do advocate just that! The ocean has more than 40 chemicals not ordinarily found in our diets. Tests even tend to show that drinking of a few teaspoons of ocean water a day can prevent cancer! The American Medical Association has not officially said that, but many of its members have convinced themselves that it is true. Often the American Med is years slow in accepting newness, or even in testing new preventives and cures.

In any event, human society today is cheating itself when it puts highly intelligent men and women workers out to pasture just because they have a few gray hairs. Yes, there are exceptions, so we must say that the decision is individual. But surely . . . surely . . . commerce and industry will benefit immeasurably when they learn how to make individual decisions, rather than arbitrarily retiring everybody at age 65. The Good News is that intelligent executives already are coming to realize that, and we can expect even more heartening changes of policy during the next decade. The average life span has moved from 50 to 75, and most of us in our 70s confidently expect to live effectively well into our 80s. I see that all around me, in my "retirement" town of 20,000.

Regardless of age or employment, though, if you "retire" your mind you will soon be whipped. You will become senile and dependent. Several research centers and many individual experts have zeroed in on this matter since 1960 or so. They have shown that beyond any doubt the human mind will in effect atrophy, waste away, unless it is kept happily stimulated and exercised. It is much like maintaining skill and efficiency in any field of endeavor (including the male's erection in anticipation of sex)—you must use it or lose it. Often said in mild jest, that admonition is really profound. Every physical and mental muscle we have must be kept healthily exercised.

PRECISELY HOW TO "EXERCISE" YOUR MIND

There are endless ways. Virtually all of them are pleasant, and most of them cost no money at all.

They can be summed up in one magnificent word—CREATIVITY.

For every person who has grown out of infancy, creativity is the divine spark of life. This seems especially true for us who are in advanced years and who have a horror of becoming senile. We all know that God is the one Great Creator; of us all, and of everything else in the universe. Very well, we are told that we are children of God, created in his image. Therefore we are impelled to be as much like him as possible, all of our lives. That means we too are obligated to be creative, within the scope of our mortal talents and potentials, which incidentally are far greater than most of us have ever imagined.

This gets us, again, to that consideration of atheists. But we have seen that atheists are merely pitiable souls guilty of self-delusion. "An atheist," some pundit has said, "is a person who writes a book proving that there is no god, then prays that it has a big sale." So in point of fact, there are no genuine atheists.

Very well, then, if the Great Creator exists, we are obligated to be as creative as we can. Creativity prevents senility.

THE CANCER OF THE SOUL

You in your trembly emotional insecurity, your anxiety about old age, may tell me in faltering voice, "But I am too *old* to do anything creative. I am a has-been. Why, do you know, I will be 72 next month?" That last said as a clincher, the snap-tone suggesting that no rebuttal is possible.

Phooey. What are you pleading for, Bertha, or Buster? Sympathy?

Truth is—in that lamentation you are simply feeling sorry for yourself. And I warn you again and again, self-pity is the most despicable personality trait that you can develop. For any person of *any* age self-pity is the cancer of the soul.

So what if you are age 72? Why dwell on it, why proclaim it? Who cares anyway? If the matter comes up, admit your age with a smile then dismiss it from your mind and get on with the happy process of living.

You also told me that you are "too old to do anything creative."

That's a lie. Even if you are in a wheelchair or if you are bedridden, it is a lie; you were still fishing for sympathy, pitying yourself. The finest of all the arts probably is creative *thinking*—did you ever consider that? "As a person thinketh, so is he." That is not the same as foolish fantasizing, daydreaming oneself into vaporous grandeurs. It means, instead, calm, constructive, upbeat attitudes. It means recognizing and appreciating the subtler nuances of life, things as trivial as a violet blossom, a ray of sunshine, a baby's smile, a canary's song. Such minutiae are, in truth, the plus factors of life! Collecting them, I was told by one elderly soul motionless from a stroke but able to mumble a few words, can make every day an exalting one. Which just may be creativity at its peak!

"IF THERE WERE DREAMS TO SELL . . ."

The creative person is a dreamer.

No, not a vapid Walter Mitty type who habitually envisions himself as a hero, but one whose sensible mind ranges far beyond the day's routine. Dreams—hopes and imaginings, based on selfless potential—are the very stuff of life, the ingredients of success and grandeur. Please, please make the distinction.

Then come right out coldly and ask yourself—"If there were dreams to sell . . . what would I buy?" I injected this thought earlier.

I have an extensive collection of literary cameos; profiles on women and men who have been creative, who have achieved, and have left indelible imprints on mankind.

One of the prettiest cameos is of Joanna Graham Bethune.

Jo's time on earth was in the long, long ago. She lived a century and a half before any such outrage as militant, activist "Women's Lib" besmirched the scene. Oh she was all for women's rights and equality, just as all intelligent folk, are today; but she would never have been sarcastic and spiteful and insulting about the matter. She will be honored in American consciousness centuries after Gloria Steinem is forgotten and moldering in her grave.

In 1816 the aging Joanna Bethune—*aging*, mind you—was honored nationally as "the creator of Sabbath Schools in America."

A creator!

A "mere" woman, still called the mother of Sunday Schools. One who performed creatively in an era when women were truly downtrodden and held not to have anywhere near the mentality of us superior males. She did not berate us as males. She did not picket the White House. Not long ago at a big banquet in Phoenix I heard Gloria Steinem refer to the President of The United States contemptuously as "that pig in the White House." The contrast is marked!

Even back in 1797, Jo Bethune in New York organized the Society for The Relief of Poor Widows—which surely, surely, was a deft push for women's rights! Not sarcastic militant aggression, but glorified creativity.

There were many other of Jo's good works, far too many to list here. Through God's grace she became *very* old for her generation, but at age 81 was still teaching a big Sunday School class!

Senile?

Joanna Bethune?

Never!

She went around our nation asking people that question I have just urged you to ask yourself—"If there were dreams to sell . . . what would you buy?"

Beautiful! In spirit and personality. Activating the two greatest words in the English language—compassion, and outreach. In the long, long ago, when opportunity for women's achievement was very poor. You modern ladies have a thousand times the opportunity that Joanna had.

"BUT I AM PHYSICALLY HANDICAPPED."

So you keep telling me. Your whining has become habitual.

Therefore I now introduce you to a famous European gentleman named Ludwig van Beethoven.

Now he had a handicap; one of the worst. Ludwig was totally deaf. Doctors and psychologists rate it worse than total blindness. I would never have agreed to that, until I myself developed almost the same handicap. My own deafness is so acute that I can understand his problems of "adjusting" and acceptance and building a new way of life, mostly around silence.

I hereby enter my own plea for sympathy, dang it all! Us "deffies" need it! Actually, of course, very little is being said today that is worth hearing, but we do miss some good sounds. And if you, sir or madam of whatever age, still have perfect hearing—count your blessings!

You cannot possibly have any conception of the intolerance that society in general has for deaf or partially deaf persons. I was astounded, to think back at my own former attitudes here. Most people have scant patience with us who are hard of hearing. Whenever a blind person happens along, everyone within range will spring to help him, to sympathize and guide. But a "deaf" person is—*funny!* Comical, heavens-to-Betsy. They make endless jokes about us, though no one ever jokes about blindness, and deafness is much worse when it comes to that priceless rapport which means "getting along with people." Even our own mates are impatient with the other mates' deafness; it is inconvenient for *them*, it is a nuisance to have to speak louder and more distinctly, or repeat statements, or write hasty messages, or remember to come close and enunciate clearly. I am recording all of these facts here because one out of every six persons past age 65 today *is* hard of hearing—and the percentage is going to get much worse, because of the raucous sounds everybody faces now.

Ludwig van Beethoven was totally deaf when he composed his immortal "Ninth Symphony," which after all these years is merely the finest possible musical score. A *deaf* man, writing music!

He triumphed *in spite of!* Creativity indeed!

LOOK NOW AT ARTHUR FIEDLER

True, Beethoven was a rarity. But if you still insist that nobody could be a distinguished musician in high old age today, I slap back at you by mentioning our own American Arthur Fiedler.

At age 82 good old Art was still conducting the Boston Pops Orchestra, one of the world's greatest. He had held that job for 45 years. He also conducted other great musical groups, around the world. More than 50 million of his records have been sold. "Oh yes, I am slowing a little," he confessed on that 82nd birthday, smiling benevolently. "Until a short time ago I was conducting 194 concerts a year. That was too many, so now I have cut them down to 164 a year."

What have YOU been doing these past few years, grand-pop-who-reads-here? Moping around, feeling sorry for yourself, damning the government and the younger generation, being a burden to your wife and other kin? Better you had died 10 years ago; our earth is already too crowded to put up with your kind. Why have you avoided creative endeavors?

Fiedler is not an isolated instance. At age 90 the great Toscanini was still conducting his orchestra. At age 89 the "unknown" Henry Lamont was conducting an orchestra in Houston, Texas—and every musician in it was past 80 years of age! They were giving regular concerts to packed houses.

The retirement town in which my beloved Adele and I now live has nine big musical groups of eager, talented singers and several more of instrumentalists. One is called simply, "The Afternooners." These fine elderly men and women get together every week day in a big room with a lot of chairs—and sing. Who leads, who "conducts?" Anybody! For the opener, maybe it will be Martha O'Clair, who used to be on the vaudeville stage singing gay melodies and kicking up her silver-slippered heels so that we young gents in the front rows could see well up past her knees—whoops! So what if Martha is now 88 years of age? She is still a vivacious vixen with verve and vitality, she declines to decline. Sometimes she sings with my friend and fellow Kiwanian who also was a topflight vaudevillian soloist in the Good Old Days, Arden Ackert, a widower with no hair and no despair, a genial gent who is the most popular man in our big Kiwanis Club. Either of those typical old Americans could have "retired" then just sat around and moped, feeling sorry for themselves. They didn't.

EVEN IF YOU ARE NOT MUSICAL—

Many other aging citizens who are nominally "retired"—write.

They "compose." Music. Books. Essays. Memoirs. Poems. Hundreds of thousands of people past 60 have enriched literature. One of them, world famous, died in 1976 when she was well into her 80s; you will recognize her name as that of the greatest mystery writer the world has ever known and she worked right up to the month of her passing—Agatha Christi.

Or consider my close friend and golf companion, Maurice "Maury" Ramsey. He is a dapper, handsome, romantic, daydreaming, immensely kind and capable elder citizen who steers his electric golf cart over to my house about once a month and reads aloud to me—his latest epic poem. And I mean, the boy is *good*. His stuff often is better than the poems of Edgar Guest, and are much in the same All-American, we-love-everybody, hearts-and-flowers mood. Maury's get published into books, too. And read from pulpits and other podiums. And quoted in newspapers and magazines. And collected by us fans of his. Maury is a past lieutenant-governor of his big Kiwanis Club District, past-president of his own Club, a sought-after speaker every week. An old gentleman, who will never be old! A *creative* senior, who will never be hampered by senility.

It is not at all imperative that you sell your writings to a publisher of magazines or books. Write your family history, and do it with verve and enthusiasm. Write the history of your town and/or country. Make inexpensive electronic copies of those manuscripts. File these in local libraries, also with kin and friends, thus leaving a far better "monument" to yourself than any hunk of chiseled marble in some graveyard. Nobody much hangs around graveyards anymore anyhow; cremation is the upcoming thing in disposing of our earthly "remains." Whoever would learn anything worth while from reading the words on your tombstone anyway? But your manuscripts can be of great help to students and researchers for centuries to come. I well know! As a professional author (more than 80 books, and some 2,000 magazine articles) I have often benefitted from the writings of men and women with such foresight, good people who set down records of life before the Civil War and on through the westward migration into this century. I owe them much. And I would bet that those authors had no senility.

SOMETHING MORE PHYSICAL?

Or maybe you prefer a more "physical" life. Okay, get up out of that rocking chair and figuratively launch your ship.

Just a few months before I wrote this page, an American gal flew across the Atlantic Ocean—alone—at age 81! Imagine! I had her name but lost it, but no matter. Who did that young spriggens Lindbergh think *he* was? He was only 27? Our gal was three times that, hence of course much too "old and feeble" to accomplish anything. Bah!

Incidentally, reports said that she *sang* her way across, because flying alone can become boring, tedious. Well, my mother used to sing when working alone all day in our farm-and-ranch garden, too. So why not? Singing is good for the spirit any time. If I were flying any daggoned contraption across the ocean, I would tend to sing hymns of praise, hoping the Lord would smile on me. Do you sing at your housework, madam, or your yard work, mister? While walking out alone or with your mate, roamin' in the gloamin', do you harmonize a little, do you hum, or whistle? Do you?

Or do you just "set" and stare off into space, dour and sour?

Creativity stretches as broad as the horizons. Consider Harry Lieberman. Harry is a Jew. I am a Gentile, but, yes, "some of my best friends"— you know. I often feel that Jewish minds are better disciplined than our Gentile minds. Surely it is an interesting fact that *the percentage of senility among Jews is markedly lower than among us Gentiles.* Perhaps that is because, in order to survive as a unified and proud people, they have *forced* themselves to be innovative, they have deliberately specialized in adaptability, they have made creativity a life routine. Thus the Disraelis, the Kissingers et al.

Harry Lieberman lived in New York state, in a town about which I have often wondered—Great Neck. Whoever named a town that? Why not something normal, like Bogaloosa, Mississippi, or El Pueblo de Nuestra Señora la Reina de Los Angeles de la Porciuncula, California? American place names are as wild as American Congressmen, and if we don't—

Where was I? I do tend to stray off . . . Oh yes, about Harry Lieberman. Well, at age 79—79, mind you—good old Harry knew absolutely nothing about art. He had never so much as dipped a brush in a bucket of paint. He had "retired" from a prosaic job, and for six years had strained to keep himself mentally alive, refusing to become a walking oyster. His stimuli included reading and high-level conversation and observing nature and meditating. One morning Henry chanced to visit the clubhouse in a retirement center; just poked in, curious. A lady latched onto him. "Here," said she brightly. "This is a paint brush. There are some oils and paper. Go sit down and try to paint a picture."

Harry Lieberman had never even painted a barn door, much less a landscape. But as I write this some years later, he has painted more than 400 primitives on themes from the Bible and the Talmud, all of which have been gobbled up by the public at good prices, and the best ones of which are on display in six major museums. Mr. Lieberman has made the most of a *second* career, launched in old age.

As I write this, Harry is exactly 100 years of age and is still painting. As a sideline, he also is helping President and Mrs. Jimmy Carter "try to teach people how to retire at age 50 and not waste their senior years feeling sorry for themselves."

If there were dreams for sale . . . what would you buy?

Dreams ARE for sale. Do not let the world pass by, you buy.

7

Creativity
For Us Common Folk

If we did all set out to buy dreams, a great many of us would buy glory.

Glory. Which translated means fame, money, status, prestige.

That reach for "position" in our competitive world is compelling. In America we all but worship "success," without pausing often enough to define it. We are so celebrity conscious that we make fools of ourselves with it—as witness how we idolize sudden prominence in actors and athletes, even in prostitutes and thieves, ignoring or forgetting that their "fame" is almost invariably a contrived thing flaunted in our faces cynically by "press agents" or public relations firms. What is your personal mature attitude about this?

Typically, a certain boy was peaceful and happy and virtually unknown, until one day in the Los Angeles Colosseum with the matchless U.S.C. Trojans he galloped for six touchdowns against mighty Notre Dame. Impossible! Nobody does that to the Fighting Irish in football. This boy did and—WHOOSH! Almost instantly the smiling halfback metamorphosed into a "celebrity" sashaying around town in one of his six expensive automobiles and one of his reputed more than 50 fine suits of clothes; public adulation had caused gifts to be showered upon him. No no, nothing illegal or even immoral, people said; just poor judgment. But *our* judgment in idolizing him was even worse! The boy had really contributed nothing to the advancement of human society, he had simply outrun a few other nice boys. Too many of us Americans—aging ones included—think that unless we are famous and rich, we are nothing. Thus emphasis is tragically misplaced.

But a great many more millions of us see through that fallacy. This group has learned true adaptability; has learned that wholesome, creative endeavors offset frustrations and failures and fears. Such folk know that any dream of glory or "fame" is not really a dream at all, rather it is a delusion. "Fame" is as unstable as a flame; and as dangerous. It can wreck—not enrich—the second half of your life.

Bethune, Beethoven, Fiedler and Lieberman were chosen here as representative people who deserved and maintained their fame. Each was—or is—a humble consecrated person. For many others the correct word is not "famous," it is "notorious." Thus the prostitutes who blatantly allege that they shacked up with certain Presidents in the White House, and hire ghost writers to produce books about their bedroom adventures there. Thus the quarterbacks and other sports figures who smirkingly boast on television and elsewhere of their "conquests" among gullible females, about their prowess as drinking companions, about anything at all that will get them attention and help increase their salaries. These and all of their ilk are *not* humble consecrated persons, in fact most of them are downright jerks. Circumstance, and press agentry, rather than superiority in life's true values, put them into the public spotlight.

If you envy those, the dream you have bought is a shallow one indeed. But the happy truth is, the vast majority of us men and women over age 40 see through all that outrageous exploitation. We decry it. We dare not act holier-than-thou moralistic about the matter, but we are a quiet force condemning such mores and manners of our time. Without us to keep American society leveled, it would be in a mess.

"GENIUS" IS NOT AN IMPERATIVE

Thus it is that we must never envy the unduly prominent. And we must never make the mistake of thinking that only geniuses can be creative achievers.

In truth, "genius" is a variable, and may command no fame at all. It can and commonly does burgeon in the humblest, least known human beings, the financially poor and the ones who might seem to have every reason to be poor in spirit.

I think of an old acquaintance with the fascinating name of Francisco Miguel Bustamente de la Falces de la Riva y Peralta; called Pancho.

Pancho is dirt poor; literally.

His home is a one-room shack of unfired adobe clay bricks. Its floor is packed desert soil. Its location is in southern Arizona, at the edge of a tiny isolated village where everyone is as humble as he.

For years Pancho earned a living for himself and his family by working as a *zanjero* (pronounced zahn-HAY-ro). This is a man who roams farm fields, often at night, turning irrigation water on and off as needed, a very lonely though important service. There, as did the shepherds of old, he made himself a little reed flute. While watching the water flow under the sun or the stars, timing it precisely, Pancho would commune with the universe, using that crude woodwind instrument. Sometimes he would lift his own voice in soft, ethereal song. Pancho Peralta, a poor but happy man.

When crippling arthritis forced him to retire physically at age 61, Pancho declined to dessicate and die. He hobbled to a chair in the warm sunshine of his village—and held court. He asked all his friends, both Latin and Anglo, please to come to him when they could find the time, and with him sing Mexican folk songs. The many kind people of his region responded.

CANTA Y NO LLORES

Upshot is, at age 81 Señor Francisco Peralta is a highly honored authority on Mexican folk music. He collected songs. Preserved them *in his mind*—mental exercise. Memorized both words and tunes.

He also extended that treasury of knowledge to others. This is very important; mental outreach, selflessness, or *un-self-centeredness*, IS AS VITAL AS ACTUAL LEARNING! Many "brilliant" scholars miss that concept. Well, no, they are not brilliant; just potentially so.

Thus it was that a long succession of girls and boys, young adults, middle-aged and elderly folk, has gathered periodically and learned to sing from and with Pancho, often under a starlit sky and a benevolent moon. In fact one of the songs especially favored by us Anglo-Americans has to do with the matchless magic of night on the desert—

> *Moonlight is beaming and starlight is gleaming,*
> *I'm dreaming of you, my Chiquita-a-a-a-a.*
> *Li-ife would be so much sweeter-er-r-r-r,*
> *In your arms, se-ñor-ri-ita-a-a-a-a-a-a-a.*

That is the English version, and that is the Mexicans' delightful way of singing it, with liquid-languid long-drawn-out musical syllables. Then the Spanish chorus is sung *fortissimo* and gloriously, faces lifted to those skies—

> *AY, AY, AY-AY,-y-y-y-y-y-y-y,* (Yes, yes yes)
> *Can-ta y no llo-res-s-s-s-s,* (Sing, and do not be unhappy)
> *Por-que cantando se alegran*
> *Ci-e-li-to lindo los co-ra-zon es-s-s-s.* (Because singing from the heart is a good thing to do).

My translation is not literal; I wanted only to convey the feeling, the mood, the deep inner sensitivity of those people. It is this that my friend Pancho engenders in all who surround him and join him in song. No wonder he is honored. No wonder this impecunious, illiterate, leather-faced, gray-haired, stooped, pain-ridden old gentleman has no hint of senility, but is radiant of spirit, an inspiration to all who know him. Dreams were for sale, and he bought a grand one.

ELOPEMENT WITH ADELE

To express it another way—dear humble un-famous

beloveds—when you "retire" do not just sit there, DO SOMETHING!

Let me enlarge on that by getting personal. As a youth I bought a dream. It was personified in a very wonderful college co-ed. She was the campus beauty. Every clunk of a football captain and other campus hero at Rice University panted after her. I too panted, skinny shitepoke that I was.

Don't ask me how, but somehow I won. Whoever understands the chemistry of love? So when she got her diploma, we eloped. Whoops! Her Mom flipped her own lid about that; Mom had envisioned a big church wedding, and predicted that our wedding wouldn't last because we had "run away." Perhaps she was right; Adele and I have been happily wed for a mere 52 years so far; something might wreck us yet—hey? Like, if I make a fool of myself sometime. But meanwhile we have celebrated our Golden Wedding with a memorable trip through Alaska and Canada and a big reception in our hometown church, and both Adele and I are "retired" please-excuse-that-ugly-word and getting along fine, thank you.

I did not quit writing. After half a century of it I have more "ideas" for books than ever. But Adele decided to start some new interests. She was already an expert bridge player; and incidentally bridge is truly a good recreational endeavor for elders *because it is mentally stimulating*; dang it all, you just can't play bridge well without exercising your mind.

But bridge can also become an obsession; many players seem to live for nothing else, some elders playing it for hours every day. That is ridiculous. So much bridge (or any card game) is too indoorsy, too restrictive; and too often done in a horrid smoke-filled room. So what *else* is available, my Adele wondered?

She poked into a lapidary laboratory. That turned out to be a big room with dozens of saws and grinders and shakers and other equipment designed to help people cut rough pieces of marble and other stones, into what are called *objets d'art*—objects of art. You know, like Michelangelo done.

Did. Only, lapidary art usually is not on such a grand scale as that chiseled out by good old Mike. That Eye-talian boy could look at a cube of solid white marble as big as your kitchen, and inside it see a masterpiece called David or Pieta. Then he would pick up hammer and chisel, start humming and tapping, and the masterwork took form. Marvelous! Incredible! Genius for sure. A dream made tangible and real. But Adele and most of us are lesser mortals, she figured, so she worked on stones the size of a cantaloupe or a watermelon.

After a few weeks of training and making little bolo tie gemstone pretties and dainty rock butterflies on colored rock flowers for Christmas gifts to family and friends, she began working on a 13-inch-high block of black Italian marble. She gave the finished product to me.

Oh boy, I wish you could see that. It sits on our living room table, in our most honored spot. It is a Madonna and Child, in very graceful modern curve, exquisite bas relief in black marble mounted on a white marble background. It is breathtakingly beautiful. Everyone says so. Some knowledgeable person viewed it—and forthwith offered me $2,500 for the piece. I turned it down. But I warned my giddy daughters and granddaughters, who will inherit, not to take that lovely heirloom lightly.

Okay, so Adele was merely an "average housewife" who made no claim to being a genius. But—I ask you—precisely what *is* genius? I submit that it often lurks in the humblest of us, awaiting its call. In nominal retirement, Adele declined to sit and dessicate, she adapted to a new life by developing a *creative* outlet—which I hold is at least a good common garden-variety of genius, which can be matched or excelled by almost any of you who read here. The second half of her life has been the best half, or, more grammatically, it has been the better of the two.

Yours does not have to be rock work. It can be—stitchery? Oil painting? Wood carving? Macrame? Leather tooling? Mosaic tile? Piano playing? You name it! Adele had barely heard of rock carving before she went into it, so it offered the further zest of discovery and learning, it exercised her mind, challenging her to think. She is still doing fine things there; is now producing exquisite intarsias, which are rock-inlay pictures for framing or table tops. I remember seeing a table top when she and I first visited Florence. Some Italian rock hound had worked a border of climbing roses, around a lake scene with a castle and mountains. It was *so* lovely that I said to Adele, "I am going to buy that table and ship it home to Phoenix, Arizona. I don't care if it costs me $500." In my naivete, I thought I had mentioned the ultimate possible figure.

The price on it was a mere $35,000.

So, if you *must* measure worth in terms of money (which of course is foolish) then most of the nice things that you can turn out in mature-years endeavors are quite valuable. Adele works on her intarsias maybe three or four half-days a week, in pleasant surroundings with congenial fellow artists.

Meanwhile she goes hiking, she swims half a mile daily, she works hard as a deaconess in our church, she reads good books, she is active in three clubs, she cooks and keeps house, she travels the world with me. Senility? "Sorry, I just haven't found time for it," says that former Rice University co-ed, now edging well into her 70s.

Again—is my point clear?

BOB AND JEANNE

Actual case histories are important; we can all get inspiration from them. So now I invite you to consider our younger friends, Bob and Jeanne Decker. Bob is, what Adele calls a Greek-god-type—the lout! (Why wasn't *I* born with a dimpled chin and broad shoulders, like the man in the Arrow Collar ads?) He is my close friend, even though I am 15 years his senior. Jeanne—called Jan by friends—is a very ornamental piece of femininity, even though she is another all-American housewife just as you ladies who read this probably are. Jan could be your nice friend-next-door in any community, quiet and dignified and smiling—and deep.

Very early, Bob and Jan Decker took the somewhat unusual attitude that people should begin their retirement long before actual retirement time. Which, of course, is nothing less than sensible. Everything that adults do at any age should in some measure be in preparation for a better Tomorrow. And if that's a cliché—which it is—remember please that most clichés have the merit of being gospel truth.

The Deckers philosophized that *change is the greatest energizer ever invented.* Sameness is stifling. And you well know that waning energy is the Number 1 bane of the aging people. The theme song of the typical retiree is "I am tired, tired, tired, I am all worn-out." Most of that is purely mental, but is all the more potent therefore. Bob and Jan did more than discuss change, they latched onto it with zest, they adapted to it, tapped it as a source of new energy. Long before he quit his formal work they recognized the restorative energy of change and began using it.

For one thing, this "average" American couple did not let themselves be wedded to one house, one place, one environment, as millions of folk do. They did not worship the dictum that "this is where we were born and reared and this is where we will live and die." People say that as if it were the ultimate in laudable attitudes. Thus the common straining to cling to the old homestead, to buy some old barn of a mansion and "restore" it, to ferret out "antiques" and ensconce oneself among them. I submit that such people, however nice they may be, are in fact, fearful, without realizing it. They instinctively cling to Yesterday, when in point of fact the real grandeur of life is Today, with Tomorrow looming even better.

Am I being mean, in that opinion? "Judging" my fellow beings? Condemning their reverence for our American heritage? Not at all! I am simply warning you good readers that, as never before, the Forward Look is now an imperative. We must love the past, honor all that was good in it by showing that to our children, but *live* in the Now.

The Deckers did that. Among other new horizons sought by them, they began to activate their dream of foreign travel. They thought first of Europe. They reasoned that it was Europe which really begat us. From that condensed, compact civilization and collection of countries, have come our American blood lines mostly, our language, many of our modes in dress, many of our foods, our mores and manners, even our religion. "See America First" is by no means a sacred commandment; it is a chauvinistic gimmick fostered by local tour agencies and chambers of commerce and has nought to do with patriotism. If we see Europe first, we can then see America and appreciate how much we have upgraded our heritage. But old people in general do no such reasoning; they have long been brainwashed by Fourth of July orators pouring pompous platitudes.

Which pompous pontification from me, reminds me of a story!

Being reminded of a story, I remind *you*, is an inalienable right of all us elderly folk. It says so right there in the Bible, the Talmud, the Koran, the Magna Carta, and the Constitution of The United States. Or if it doesn't, it ought to, dang it all.

Well, anyhow it seems that Minnie and Buster Prototype were well up into their age 70s, and had lived all their life in cold upper Wisconsin. One dreary sleety snowy February day the old couple sat together huddled in blankets before a radiator that had icicles on it due to an energy shortage. Buster felt and looked very glum. Presently he spoke in old man's tremolo—"M-Minnie, we are g-gettin' ol. If'n one of us was to die, what would the other'n do?"

Minnie wasn't about to buy that; she had more spunk. Spunk is a colloquialism meaning pluck. Pluck is a good word meaning courage. And courage is a might important thing to have when you are old. So Minnie replied, "I don't know what you's do if I died, Bus. But if *you* died first, I know what I'd do. I'd take a long trip through the Caribbean and

Spain and southern France and Italy, then fly back and settle down to live in sunny southern California.''

Well, bless Minnie and all her kind! I live in sunny Southern Cal myself, and frankly we don't *need* more immigrants, we got too many people here already, we wish you rich easterners would come out as tourists, spend a lot of money, then hightail it on back home. But I respect Minnie's adrenalinized get-up-and-go, her refusal to be wedded to her past, her eagerness to make the most of newness and change. Which is also why I am parading Bob and Jan Decker before you, as my real-life couple who recognized the creative stimuli in travel. They agree with me that ''A month in Europe is worth a year in college.''

TOTAL AND ABRUPT CHANGE

Although well entrenched in sales of heavy construction equipment in California, Bob ''changed'' by phasing into a second career. He accepted a challenging offer involving the introduction of an American product to the construction and mining industry in Europe, the Middle East, and Africa. That change in the lives of the Deckers was total and abrupt. From a comfortable ranch-style home in California's San Joaquin Valley they moved into a diminutive 16th century cottage in a small village located in the green belt west of London.

Now, you might argue that they went backward; from modern California to ancient England village life. And it is true that the English in general make fools of themselves with their worship of the past, their idolization of Yesterday. Heavens, if a house there wasn't built at least back in the 16th century, and preferably the 13th, it is hardly worth noticing! (I am exaggerating; England does have its clan of modern folk, but the old heads remain Victorian.) ''Right on this spot,'' a tour guide told my Adele and me in a musty drafty old ''cahstle'' in rural England, ''is where the owner, Sir Gawain himself, was stabbed to death by his wife's lover. There—you can still see his bloodstains on the hearth. It happened in the year 1581.'' Big deal! The smug Limey made a mountain out of that molehill of history.

But hark—those are the mores and manners of the British! They *like* such reverence for the past; they cling to past glories in economics, military prowess, social prestige, all that. Which undoubtedly is why Britain is—sad to relate—virtually a dying nation. The once great "Empiah" on which the sun never set, today is a frightened, bankrupt little clutch of very loveable people huddled on tiny islands off the shore of France. A major tragedy of the 20th century! A heartbreak for all the civilized world.

Knowing all that—Bob and Jan Decker pitched in to *study* England. Is that point clear, dearly beloveds? When you travel, do not for heaven's sake just haunt the posh Hilton Hotel lobbies and the garish night clubs; get out among The People, the villages and small towns. Get the *feel* of the nation, the emotional content. The Deckers did precisely that. They proved that the surest immunization against further shock, is knowledge! One form of that is an abiding heart interest, *a participating part in the mores of the people in any foreign land visited*. Participating, mind you; not just observing. This cannot be overly emphasized.

Very soon, the Deckers became captivated. They were charmed by the English way of life. They developed lasting friendships with their fellow villagers. Without realizing it at first, they even began speaking in English idiom and accent—"Ah theah, old chap; I siy, aren't the flahs lovely this morning?" What? Flahs, I myself had to learn, is the correct English way of pronouncing *flowers;* we of the Colonies don't know that! Bob and Jan were soon unconsciously saying "O-oh no-oh" for "Oh no." And calling the hood of their car a "bonnet." And referring to the mail man as "Postie." Well well, what fun! Before they realized it, those two upper-middle-class Americans were *in*. Accepted. Admired. Even loved.

Bob's work required constant travel. So, in his absence Jan immersed herself in activities that were unique to England. One such new interest was Brass Rubbing.

BRASS RUBBING? WHAT'S THAT?

Whoever rubs brass, for goodness sake? I remember how saloon keepers and hotel flunkies used to have to rub brass doorknobs and brass spittoons into mirror-like shininess, when those conveniences were thought to be imperative, back in the halcyon Days of Yore. But what in tunket could a modern dainty refined American housewife do rubbing brass in Merrie England?

Well, it seems that many of the ancient churches in those villages have brass engravings embedded in their stone floors, under pews, on walls, behind organ lofts, or almost anywhere else within the confines of the cathedral, any space large enough to sustain a larger-than-life-sized monument. Strictly English! I know of nothing comparable in America.

The brasses there depict and memorialize important personages who lived as far back as the 13th and 14th centuries—here we go, preserving that antiquity, seemingly obsessed with it. Anyhow, it was *those* brasses that Jan Decker rubbed.

The art of Brass Rubbing requires a small supply of high rag-content paper available at any art supply store, also a wax crayon called a "heelball" don't-ask-me-why which is similar to a substance used by Picadilly Circus bootblacks to blacken sole edgings. (Whoo!) Masking tape also is required, to hold the paper in place over the brass. Needed also are a soft brush to clean the brass plate, and plenty of elbow grease (is there anyone present who doesn't know what elbow grease is?) as well as a penchant for kneeling—not necessarily in supplication.

Figure the average rubbing time to be about two hours. "The nicest thing about Brass Rubbings," says Jan, "is that you meet such nice people—literally in church." Some of Jan's rubbings are worthy of display in museums. Her enthusiasm bespeaks the finer nuance of creativity, and of adaptability.

"A CULTURAL FEAST"

She did not allow herself to become a one-interest person. When not prowling through village churches, she painted scenes of the English landscape in water colors and oils. All of England is exceedingly picturesque, as any traveler there will testify. "Living there is a cultural feast," says Jan.

During the weekends when Bob was home, visits were made to museums, art galleries, concerts, theatrical productions, and village fairs. They especially enjoyed the London theaters. New York City likes to think that it is the theatrical center of the universe. Hollywood insists that *it* is. But in point of fact, London excels all others—and saying so does not make me an Anglophile and does not lessen my American patriotism.

Other English towns and villages are "high" on Theater also. The greatest playright of all times was born and lived out his life just a few miles up country from London, you know. The Deckers sensed all these things as Opportunity. They moved into the life streaming there, sampling the richness of history, the grandeur of the arts. They do grieve, because as I said, England is in a sad sad state politically and economically. But then—have we Americans cause for comparable worry and grief about our nation? Chicanery in Washington and inflation everywhere here are endangering us as well.

Bob's business took him to exotic places far from the trails of tourists. He made repeated trips to the mining sites of Norway north of the Arctic Circle; to the diamond mines of Kimberly, South Africa; to construction sites in the Trucial States of Saudi Arabia; to deep mines in the African jungles; and to places as far afield as northwest Australia, where some of the richest iron ore deposits in the world exist. While in Australia side trips were made to the Great Barrier Reef, also to an aborigine reservation on Groot Island in the Gulf of Carpentaria.

Bob and Jan Decker returned to America in 1973 after

almost eight fulfilling and enriching years that have renewed their lives beyond all measure. Soon after their return they discovered Leisure World in Laguna Hills, California, where they took up residence.

But for them, the word "retirement" does not exist, and never will. Every day toward sundown I encounter them in one of our huge beautiful swimming pools. There we not only plow through the cool water or relax in the 106-degree swirling pool, we "visit." We and others swap talk on the day's activities, which are legion. A gathering! A fellowship! A spontaneous, happy forum.

Should you envy us?

Absolutely, you should. We would welcome you. I have detailed the experience of the Deckers, because most of you who read here will have a degree of affluence, and can work out something comparable for yourselves; some broadening look at the whole earth and not just your little hometown niche. Travel! Mingle with folk in other lands. Do not spout "ugly Americanisms at them," *listen* to them, then gently do your own sharing. How else can we folk of earth build that idealistic One World of which our leaders speak? Doing, in effect, what the Deckers did, is high-level creativity which you can match or excel in your own way. Which is why I have detailed the Deckers for you. Incidentally, as I write this they have just departed for Hawaii, on a happy two-months swap-house arrangement.

HOW HIGH IS YOUR "A.Q.?"

We can say, then, that "creativity" is simply a happy reach-out for excellence, a working to improve one's AQ—Achievement Quotient. You need not strive to be exactly like the notables, or like my wife Adele, or like the energetic Deckers. Do your *own* thing. You can upgrade your personal AQ in literally hundreds of ways.

Let us assume, for instance, that you cannot travel. Then what?

Well, you can be creative in simple home gardening.

Raising a few flowers at first, then perhaps specializing in exotic rare ones, is always rewarding. What more beautiful could anyone produce than a big bouquet of roses? Rose lore alone is a full lifetime study, and many persons have made it so. So is the study of ground flowers such as the pansies and the shy violets. Flowering trees are a wonderful speciality, where you have the space. Vine culture also opens a whole new botanical field.

Or maybe as an amateur botanist you would enjoy that truly fascinating art which the Orientals call Bonsai—pronounced *bone-sigh*.

This is the raising of *miniature* shrubs and trees, many with flowers. They are breathtaking in their beauty; exquisite works of living art; real trees, mind you, only six inches to two feet or so high, growing in dishes on living room tables—and often more than 300 years of age!

Incredible. And intriguing for sure. Such a novelty outlet in aging years can be immensely stimulating. I repeat—the correct word, *Bonzai*, which is usually heard in a shout, meaning "HURRAY!" or similar, and is spelled with a z instead of an s. Spinoff knowledge from any endeavor is always pleasing. I know at least four couples who, in their senior years, have become Bonsai specialists, giving fine lectures on the art, showing slides, teaching others; and quite incidentally, making money at it. "Senility" does not even enter their minds as a potential. Neither does boredom.

THE CAMERA CLAN

Aging Americans in ever greater numbers have also been "taking up" photography. Camera clubs or clans now flourish in almost all retirement centers, and millions of individuals are studying this art.

Give it thought; even as a sideline to the other activities if you wish. Color photography today is virtually perfect. And never you think that "taking pictures" is not an art! It is. Sad to relate, at least 99 percent of *all* photos made by the people at large, are sheer junk. Kids and oldsters alike grab cheap little drugstore cameras (which are abominations) then run around going snap, snap, snap. If the pictures "come out" at all they usually are vague, poorly focused, poorly composed. They purport to show Niagara Falls, but Henry and Susie and Cousin Wilberforce and his wife and a garbage can or a trash barrel are so prominent in the foreground that you can barely see the water. Junk. We pose our loved ones close to the camera, grinning self-consciously, in poor lighting, just to prove that we were *there*. This wholly normal, powerful urge in us mortals, has made Eastman Kodak and other camera companies immensely wealthy. But it also has stifled true beauty and art. If you are old enough to be reading this book at all, you are mature enough to understand beauty and art.

You do need a reasonably good camera, so avoid the "cheapies." If money is a main concern for you, then advertise for a good *used* camera; thousands of persons bought them, used them a few times—and now they gather dust on some upper closet shelf. Go after one of those. I myself rate as an expert scenic photographer. I have sold dozens of photos to big magazines, at fat fees, often illustrating my own writings. Also I recently had a 30-day showing of 20 color enlargements in the lobby of a big bank, with endless commendations for them. All were taken on a compact camera which sold new for about $500; I paid $80 for my used one, in perfect condition.

However—!

Note this carefully: cameras do not take pictures, *people* do!

The art is not in lens power, not solely in light-meter jigglings and all that. The art is in COMPOSITION. Knowing, or sensing, not merely how to take a photo, but WHAT to take. And what to leave out.

Approached with that in mind, photography is among the finest of the creative arts. And one of the least expensive in terms of money and time.

WHAT MAKES A GOOD PHOTOGRAPH?

The only tenable criterion I know is—instinct. This is developed by study and practice, and it will come rather rapidly if you give it a chance. I took my cue from something that the great 19th-century artist, Eugene Delacroix, said—"Any picture should above all be a feast for the eyes."

And here—again!—I am reminded of a story!

It seems that a sweet little girl gave the world the ultimate art criticism. She was in a very super-duper Museum of Modern Art, the hoity-toity kind, whose patrons feel far superior to us mere mortals who snap photos of mountains and seascapes and pretty flowers.

She was standing spread-legged before a six-foot painting of splashy greens, blues, whites and such, all in a weirdly geometric jumble. Hands on hips, she gazed up at it, entranced.

The fat-and-factuous curator of the museum spied her. He ambled over, smiled condescendingly from his lofty sophistication and said, "That, darling" is supposed to be a beautiful pony galloping across a prairie."

Whereupon little 6-year-old sweetie pie let him have it. She turned around, glared up at the curator and demanded, *"Well, why ain't it, then?"*

No, you do not have to be precisely "photographic" in recording beauty on your sensitized film; you can go modernistic, impressionistic, even surrealistic if you wish. Also, you can take good photographs from a wheelchair, even from a bed, if you are restricted. In short, the sky is the limit in taking photos.

But I do remind you—any picture should above all be a feast for the eyes.

GET OUT OF THAT ROCKING CHAIR!

You can be "creative" at the game of tennis.

Now tennis is rather strenuous, hence *of course* nobody over age 50 should ever play that game. Even as I write this, the morning paper portrays lovely Tracy Austin as the stand-out feminine tennis player of the year—and she is barely age 14. So of course if you are past 50, you must henceforth take life easy and forget about running across a cement court to whap a rubber ball with a racquet. Let me help you from your couch to your softly-padded rocking chair, grandpop or grandmom with the tremolo voice and the shaky hands.

Poppycock. Get out of that supine position, you old coot, and restore those muscles. Go to a reputable physician— not one of the too-many modern mollycoddlers who cater to your fancied feebleness and your introverted fears; and your pocketbook. Let a good man check out your blood pressure, your heart, whatever. Pay him for it without grousing. Chances are 9 in 12, the survey shows, that any person past age 50 is not only physically fit for an active and even somewhat strenuous physical life, but would greatly benefit by maintaining one.

Tennis is a creative sport.

You have to think in order to play it well. You have to be aggressive at it, not namby-pamby passive; have to think *positively* in the Norman Vincent Pealian fashion. Big Bill Tilden, the world's star tennis player of our youthful days and possibly the greatest one ever, once said, "In tennis, the first sign of old age is when you start playing a *defensive* game." So move into it, Bertha and Buster. Charge! Attack! You will be attacking potential senility when you do.

WHAT ABOUT GOLF?

Much the same thing can be said about the game of golf. It is never as good as tennis, because it is too lazily passive, kills too much time, is too costly and too frustrating to sensitive souls. Even so, it has its place. You do have to think a little to play a fair game of cow-pasture knocking-a-ball-around. But the compulsive golfer is much like the compulsive bridge player; tends to over-do it, neglecting other outlets. Avid golfers are like avid horseback riders; they seem eternally to talk of nothing but their sport, thereby alienating the affections of people with broader mental horizons. Golf is good, and good for you, but it is NOT the best sport for physical conditioning. Best take it as a sometime thing, with other activities as well. It is only mildly creative, if any.

Almost certainly at this point, some reader is going to wonder, "What about shuffleboard?" Somebody always asks that, whenever any person is lecturing on old-age activities.

My personal answer is: shuffleboard is for people who like to or have to "shuffle," which Webster defines as "moving with a dragging gait without lifting the feet." Well, phooey. If for physical reasons, you *have* to shuffle along through life—God bless. Shuffling along is better than being completely immobile, surely, and no shame, no embarrassment is attached to that form of locomotion. But most of you readers here, perhaps 99 and 44/100 percent of you, do NOT have to shuffle. You DO have the ability to walk and move about with something akin to normal gait, in fact most of you can run and jump and do most active things. Especially you who are middle-aged.

For you—shuffleboard is zilch. Zilch is a grandson idiom meaning no good, vapid, tepid, uninteresting, dull. Oh yes, there is much "science" in skilled shuffleboard playing, and big tournaments are held. But it should never have been allowed to become the symbol of retirement that it is. It is a weakling game. If you can possibly do something with more zip-and-go, more physical output, more challenge to muscle and brain—do it! Let shuffleboard wait until you get *old*. Like, maybe, when you are 91 or 92. Be guided by your physician. Somehow I can't see much creativity in shuffleboard; it seems primarily a lazy person's game. (Don't get mad! You asked, and I answered.)

THE CRUSTY FRIEND

One afternoon a while back in our swimming pool, a crusty old gaffer kept griping verbally about almost everything around our retirement town. He had been doing that for weeks; a chronic grouch.

Suddenly another man tore into him—"Look, mister, if

you dislike everything around here so much, why don't you just move your carcass out so we appreciative folk won't have to put up with you? You are trying to pursue happiness by running backward."

That shook him. That knocked him speechless. The eight men around us all remained silent, slightly embarrassed. Then the tough one softened his approach and spoke again— "Look, mister, in many ways we all agree with you. But just grousing won't accomplish anything. Tell you what—let's both get showered and dressed, and I'll take you and your wife out to dinner tonight. Okay?"

And I'll be cow-kicked if the old grouch didn't bust out bawling.

Started blubbering right there; a man well past 70. Some nice chap dried his face with a towel and said let's get out of this water, then on the deck he poked his hand at the first speaker and said, "I accept your invitation to dinner. I will be honored to dine with you. I apologize to all of you. I am a damn fool."

That's when big Bob Decker spoke up; the same Bob about whom I have told you earlier in this chapter. Bob's voice was gentle and kind. "We are all damn fools at times, Mr. Williams. Think nothing of it. Have a good time at dinner, all of you. See you here in the pool tomorrow."

Outreach! Reaching out, to touch a life. Share your life! Next day we guided Jim Williams (which is not his real name) into our vast wood-working shop in our Leisure World community. He took to it at once. Now, 10 months later, his exquisite carvings are on display in store show windows, and Jim is a happy, creative gentleman well liked by all of us. Working with his hands and mind on wood had gotten him out of himself, and re-focused his thoughts on goodness rather than badness. Woodworking is a potential outlet for almost every aging person, or even every young one, and it can be very creative indeed. But helping a troubled man is the most creative of all.

Is THAT point clear?

CREEPIE-CRAWLIES IN THE TIDE POOLS

I also know a sweet school teacher who retired and moved into our town near the Pacific shores. All her life she had worked hard, sharing her mental and physical energies with American youth. Now she just sat down, saying she wanted to rest forever. Said she had earned her right to take life easy.

Well, she hadn't.

Nobody ever earns such a right. In fact no such right exists. Life was never meant for loafing, no matter what your years. Life was never meant to be "easy," meaning inactive, unproductive, dull. In brutal fact, life for ALL of us is full of troubles and burdens, almost every week. But the happiest fact of our existence is—God never gives any of us a burden which we are unable to carry. Any failure to carry yours will be of your own making; you and I and all of us are expected to *rise above* our troubles.

"Stop that kind of malarkey," I grinned at ex-schoolmarm Margaret Devore. "I happen to know that you enjoyed a very fine, active life in the school years. If you cease all mental interests now, we will have to bury you prematurely. Or you will bury yourself in boredom and senility. Now get up out of that chaise lounge, kiddo."

Kiddo?

You young spriggenses won't know the term, but "kiddo" was hot-stuff slang for any girl we admired back in the nineteen-teens. And she remembered.

"Like what will I do then?" she demanded, in mock indignation.

"Like you will go down to our fine library and check out six books on marine biology. Then like taking the free bus every other day into Laguna Beach, 12 minutes. Then like poking into those beautiful little moss-greened tide pools among the smooth rocks at low tide, studying the fascinating life of tiny creatures there. Like learning the vast importance of the oceans in all our lives, seeing the majesty of the tides and the waves, the beauty, the power." I let her have it, but good.

She did go to the library. She took my advice! Any person who takes my advice is smart—I keep telling my grinning grandchildren; the louts. Marge was one of the rare ones who did. Next week she showed Adele and me the books she had borrowed. "One of these," she held it up, smiling, "is titled *Marvels of The Sea and Shore*. Ever hear of it?"

Yes, I had heard of it. I had written it, some years before.

"You were right," she went on. "Sea life is fascinating. I had no idea! I had always lived far inland. Now I am a happy beachcomber. I go there almost every day. How can I ever thank you?"

She didn't need to thank me. Nobody does. We all help each other, and if anything I am more indebted than deserving, I can never, never even begin to give adequate thanks to the people who have helped me through life.

Two years have passed. Margaret Devore, Ph.D., retired school teacher, is now lecturing three mornings a week in a nearby community college—on marine biology. At age 73 she looks 10 years younger and 20 years happier than when she first plopped her too-fat posterior onto that chaise lounge. Incidentally, climbing over and through seashore rocks has even reduced that posterior; spinoff benefits from any creative endeavor can be very rewarding, I keep reminding you.

BE-ATITUDE

In the final analysis, all creativity, all refusal to become "old" and unloveable even to yourself, is simply a matter of developing the proper inner control or attitude.

But you have to make it a *be* attitude. You have to *be*-gin, have to *be* up-and-doing, have to *be* in control. The very word *be*atitude means blessedness, or happiness of the highest kind. Maybe we people past age 40, offered endless new knowledge and opportunities, now need a new official Beatitude—*Blessed are ye who take charge of your lives and discipline yourselves forever, for ye shall know grandeur and peace.*

8

Your Good Health;
Or Lack Of It

Moving into the new life-style that all of us face, adapting
to changing health conditions is a major consideration.
Health is changing? It certainly is! For everybody. New
preventive techniques, new cures, new surgical methods,
better understanding of physical, mental and emotional
needs—every week we hear or read about such progress. We
who are aging have to stay alert, but sometimes the newness
does upset us. Typically—when my first daughter was born,
mother Adele was pampered in a hospital bed for 10 days;
could barely be allowed to lift a spoon to feed herself. But
this very week as I peck at my typewriter for you, a modern
young matron friend of ours had her baby one 10 a.m.,
walked down the hospital hall to show it to us at 4 p.m., and
two days later brought it happily home. "Times" have
changed—dear me!

In this informal and friendly book visit with you I have
neither the space, the need nor the inclination to offer a
detailed study of all the health problems that beset people in
the second half of their lives.

Those problems are highly individual.

Yours are not mine. Mine, of course, are infinitely more
important and appealing than yours—have I shown you the
scars from my hernia operations? They are in a fascinating
area.

Meanwhile, old buddies and girls, there *are* a few health
generalities to which we must pay serious heed. This is a
requisite for that adaptability I keep stressing. Literally, many

of us *have* to adapt to both physical and mental restrictions as we age along. The happy aspect is that we can do so with good grace and spirits.

OLD CHIEF IRONSIDE, FOR HAPPY INSTANCE

If, for example, your legs have been twisted by polio, then God bless, and I admonish you to pop that wheelchair around with all the flourish and verve and emotional guts that have been so hearteningly portrayed on television for us by the talented actor Raymond Burr in his long, successful drama series titled *Ironside.*

If you are one of the few English-speaking elders on earth who have never seen one of those clean, entertaining, hour-long dramas, then know that the aging Robert Ironside is the hypothetical Chief of Detectives in the City of San Francisco. He has an improbably beautiful and brilliant girl assistant Officer, matched by two equally unlikely young male Officers, one of them a Negro. The stories, the action, the dialogue, always are clean. Many baffling crimes come to whip his wheelchair around that city directing the solution of those crimes! Self-pity? Gooey sympathy from his underlings and other associates? Never! The creators of that program had a good hunch; handicapped viewers everywhere honor them for having Chief Bob perform with dignity and skill in that wheelchair. So do the rest of us.

All right, then. If you have *any* sort of inescapable handi-cap, my prayer and petition for you is to make the best of it. Firm up your will power, smile big, and adapt! You can do just that.

THE ADMONITION IS AUTHORITATIVE

At this point please allow me to inject a little gem that emphasizes the transcendent importance of adapting, something *really* authoritative and enduring and common-sensible for us all.

Dr. Roger Granville Caldwell once was the distinguished Dean of Students at a school famous for its academic excellence, Rice University in Houston. At the opening of one autumn semester there he told the student body—"Learn all you can from our professors and textbooks, yes. But above all else, learn the value of adaptability. Learn how you must adapt to temptations, pressures, problems and excitements that *new developments in adult life* are sure to throw at you. If necessary, forget everything else that we teach you here, but do learn controlled adaptability, how to triumph in morality and excellence and peace of mind, no matter what develops. This will be especially important in your older years."

Most of you did not attend Rice University. I did. And I printed that quotation from Roger Caldwell, Ph.D., in the school newspaper which I edited shortly after World War I. The quotation is still remembered and honored there. The truth of it has enriched my life, and that of the campus beauty with whom I eloped. Actually, adapting is the hallmark of every happy, successful person on earth.

GRACIOUS GRACE

Ironside of course is fictional, even though authentic. So let us now look at a very real person, whose name is Grace Armstrong.

Grace is well into her 70s. A widow, she lives alone. She cleans, cooks, sews, reads, listens to fine music, studies birds and flowers, makes a very fine life for herself and is much loved by a host of friends. As her greatest talent, I rate her ability—and inclination—to bake a big batch of sugar cookies every few weeks; invariably I get a platter of those! So do other people. Folks are forever dropping in because they sense the kindliness of this woman. Grace Armstrong literally Shares Her Life. Do you, gentle reader? Do I?

She lives all day every day in a wheelchair. I do not remember why, nor does it matter here. Somehow, around her is an aura of spiritual strength, which is the ultimate in wisdom. For developing wisdom, adversity can be better than university.

This is all that I am going to say about physically handicapped people except to add—whatever yours is now, or may become, just take charge and adapt.

OUR ASPIRIN CIVILIZATION

But for all of us citizens aged 40 to 100, countless other health problems arise. Because they are individual, no counseling about most of them can be offered here. In other words—do not call me; take two aspirin tablets and drop by my home tomorrow. Perhaps I can then give you a pep talk.

Ours in America is an aspirin civilization. Sometimes I even think we have an aspirin religion. That drug does have a place, but it is a very minor one, it cures nothing, it can in fact delude you by lessening pain when you really need medical attention immediately. So do avoid most aspirin intake, and all other self-doctoring, including the myriad "patent" medicines that do little but make their manufacturers rich. "Bayer" is not a synonym for God. Neither is "Geritol" or "Vicks" or "Gelusil" or "Preparation H" or "Ex-Lax" or any other proprietary medicine name. Yet millions tend to worship them more than they worship the Almighty!

We are of course brainwashed by that confounded miracle lurking in our dens and living rooms—the TV set. When a lovely young matron (a highly paid actress) comes on the screen, leans her heavenly head onto her handsome young husband's shoulder and says, "When you have your health you have just about everything, so we take Bleep ev-ry day," it is a powerful sales gimmick. We tend to run down and buy bottles of Bleep. Most of Bleeps, however, are simple concoctions of alcohol and water and maybe some vitamin B, scarcely better than the branch-water-and-whiskey cure-alls peddled to us 80 years ago by Medicine Show "doctors" from the backs of itinerant wagons; abetted by a blackfaced banjoist.

No, I am not a cynic. Yes, I do try to be realistic, and allow no self-delusion. We Americans, Canadians, English and

Australians who are past age 40, *should* be informed enough to defend ourselves, because we have access to accurate information that our forefathers lacked.

So, beloveds, do establish a sensible personal health program, by going once or twice a year to a reputable physician for a complete examination. And do be guided by his counsel, not by the come-on charlatans who advertise. What good is new knowledge if we refuse to use it—I ask you?

CLEANLINESS IS NEXT TO—

Extensive studies of aging men and women and their health problems, have revealed some surprising further facts. One is that millions of us tend to be unclean.

You heard me—unclean! Dirty! Unsanitary!

You would be astounded at how many elderly folk rarely take a bath. We try to pretend that the horrid invisible little creepie-crawlies called germs, microbes, bacteria, viruses, or whatever you want to name them, do not exist. We tacitly deny that they wriggle around inside us and cause diseases; and that they revel in uncleanliness.

Psychologists and physicians postulate that our indifference to these microscopic dangers stems from the universal ignorance which held during our childhood years. For most of us past 70 or so, germs had not been invented when we were in grade school, hence we have a hangover tendency not to believe in them now.

Invented?

All right—discovered. Because of course they were lurking around us all the time—though some of us feel that they are indeed inventions of the devil. Many an oldster today still resents them. These folk can't *see* the danger, so it doesn't exist!

My own father's attitude was like that, and was very typical of mankind's beliefs about such matters during the Victorian era and for jillions of years before. Thus it furnishes valuable background knowledge—and a warning—for us in the enlightened Today.

Papa was born in a backwoods cabin during the Civil War. Son of a secessionist, in 1910 he still had the feeling that dangerous germs were indeed invented, and by the damn yankees at that. You couldn't see them, could you? Well, then. How could anything too small to see do you any possible harm, unless it was conceived by the despised fiends Up North? Logical!

You think I am exaggerating there? Being facetious? Not at all. You modern young folk can have no idea how categorical and bitter and uneducated and naive many folk were in that era, North as well as South. My dad had attended a tiny school in a wilderness for just six weeks—the sum total of his formal "education." So he grew up with the "knowledge" that anything was clean and pure if it was white, and dirty and dangerous if it was black. Tragically, this standard often was applied to people as well as inanimate things. In the home farm routine, if a blob of cow manure dropped into the pail of milk, strain it out with a white cloth and the milk was pure again. No, no, and no, young friend, I am not exaggerating.

Papa was 60 years of age before my brother Grady, who had been sent through university and medical school, came home with an M.D. degree and a microscope. He showed papa some living germs swimming around in our freshly squeezed-out milk, and explained why they were dangerous. It was hard new knowledge; but to his credit, Papa accepted it.

"WASH YOUR HANDS!"

"After all," he reasoned aloud to us there in small-town Henderson, Texas, that distant day, "we sent Grady off to learn new truth, and we would be fools not to benefit by what he learned, I vow. From now on we scald every bucket we use for milking our cows, and we wash off the cows' teats as well as our hands."

Revolutionary! Upsetting! But new knowledge always is.

But to this day, late in the century, many older gents and

gals barely rinse their hands before preparing and eating food.

They have been horsing around town all morning, maybe playing golf or gardening or cleaning house or whatever, then they go into their kitchens, slice bread, handle salads and meats, spoons, knives, forks, plates, glasses, with hands that positively are coated with potential dangers for us. And think nothing of it. Then wonder why, a few days later, they "come down with something," such as a cold in the nose, a sore throat, a gripe in the bowels. True, we cannot allow ourselves to become compulsive-finicky about cleanliness, but we surely must set up some kind of minimal routine for it.

New knowledge tells us positively that the horrid sniffly drippy sneezy drainy achy cold-in-the-head is *not* spread to us by open windows or by sneezings from a person who has a cold. We get ours *only* from contact with a person who has a cold, or by touching things that one has used. Such as towels, napkins, drainboards, utensils, anything at all. The disease is caused by a virus, and is NOT spread through sneezings, the scientists now declare. "Close that window!" we oldsters still yelp. "Where were you born—in a barn! You will give us all a cold in the head." No such. Scientists now know that the temperature of the outside or inside air had no relation to the "cold" in your system, the virus disease that clogs your nose and sinuses for weeks. Repeat—the latter is caused only by a virus that is not airborne. But it does lurk wherever the victim has blown his nose or dripped saliva, hence his very fingers are dangerous to us. Yet how many millions of parents will kiss and cuddle a sweet child, when either parent or child has a head cold? Love does not counteract germs.

Such new knowledge is hard for us hardheaded oldsters to take. Our own mothers told us what was what about sickness, and her memory is sacred. She could not possibly have been wrong . . . could she?

It is precisely that kind of old-hat attitude that tends to cause many unnecessary ailments in old people. Also there are countless other ways in which we are unsanitary, unclean.

For further indelicate instance—new research revealed—millions of us use toilet paper, then stand up and walk away without even thinking to wash our hands. Or if we do, we make a mere ritualistic pass at washing; we dribble a little water on our fingers, swipe them on a towel thereby infecting it, and go merrily on our way. The next towel user gets any infection.

Sadly, millions of people just aren't clean.

EXERCISE! "WHO, ME?"

The sly, wisecracking members of society in my retirement town have come up with many cute bits about our life here. Just yesterday neighbor Bill Hauser got my hackles up—

"Did you hear that they are going to change the name of our Leisure World?"

"No!" I always fall for Bill's sallies. "Why are they? I like this name. What will the new name be?"

"Four Cs," replied Bill.

"Four Seas? We are near only one sea, the Pacific."

"Not that kind. C! Capital letter C. Four Cs—Canes, Crutches, Cadillacs and Cardiacs."

All right, so I was had. But a moral lurks there, too. Our town is affluent. Thus it is also—lazy. And the tendency of lazy aging people is to get too soon into canes, crutches and cardiacs.

The preventive exercise comes more naturally to the persons under age 40; family life, and body chemistry, seem to demand it. After 40 we develop a tendency to—sit. But as the fine old spiritual warns us, "You'll never get to heaven in a rocking chair." Habitual sitting (loafing, lazing around) will not only stifle your morality, it will speed up your approach to that Other Less Attractive Place. Every authority on aging stresses this fact.

The exercise must be of your own choosing. I have already praised tennis and golf, but yours can range from simple walking through jogging, swimming, calisthenics, gardening, housework, mountain climbing, boating, almost literally anything that keeps your body in lively motion. Do be guided by your physician; especially if you are over weight, as you probably are.

"WHAT'S FOR DINNER?"

In all of the nation's middle-class or luxury retirement centers 11 out of every 12 old people are too fat.

They habitually eat too much, often as pleasure—compensation for boredom or other troubles, just as they also drink too much alcohol. Every day the big pool where I swim attracts about 300 elders to its waters. Eight or ten of those are so grossly enormous as to be repulsive. They weigh more than 300 pounds. At least 20 more will top 250, and many more range from 180 to 200.

The weights are smaller for the "average" oldsters and the ones who have less money. These simply can't afford pamperings—which may be one of poverty's few blessings. Even so, many poor people manage to eat too much also, hence look slobby like their rich colleagues.

I shall offer you no easy way to reduce; no drug suggestions, no fancy body massage or roller gadget or gymnasium techniques. The cold truth is, you gain weight only by overeating, and you lose weight only by dieting down. Like it or not, there is no alternative. Stay fat, and your life expectancy will be shortened, also your life enjoyment. Stay slender and you will not only outlive the slobs, you will enjoy the process much more than they do. Statistics prove it.

Start no diet without the guidance of your trusted physician. This is very important. You need a complete "physical" before plunging into grapefruit-and-buttermilk or whatever. Let no friend "prescribe" a reducing diet, no magazine or book or lecturer or food store; to insure your survival and success, let your doctor do it. This is contrary to general folk custom; almost literally every newspaper and magazine every day dings at us with "How To Reduce" propaganda, brainwashing us into dangerous wasting of time, money and hopes. You *might* get by with their prescriptions, but also you might die. Do not be victimized.

SPACE FOOD!

About 6,000,000 elderly Americans are *mal*nourished. Most of these are loveable folk who are simply too poor to buy adequate food.

For those, man's trips to the moon and other space gallivantings have proved to be a boom. Strange! But I have already listed several other spinoff benefits from the National Aeronautics Space Administration (NASA) scientific studies, and now here is another.

To feed our space tourists, NASA developed packaged meals that not only were nourishing, balanced, and appetizing, but were delicious.

Wherefore, in 1976-77 "Meal System For The Elderly" was developed from that technical knowledge about space food. This boon was originated by the Texas Governor's Committee on Aging, and given an intensive four-month test on 168 elderly folk. Success of the test was very heartening.

Upshot is, our indigent elders everywhere soon will be able to receive well balanced, tasty, "square" meals for less than $2 each, and the federal government is almost certain to include that cost in its already Socialistic policies; or if not, the states will. The meals will arrive at each needy person's home in attractive packages, by mail or comparable parcel delivery.

Menus vary from roast beef and chicken to frankfurters and beans, chili and cottage cheese, fresh fruits and salads, cakes and pies. Each is scientifically balanced for health-giving nutrition. Any elderly person can prepare most of those free meals simply by quick heating, often by merely adding a cup of hot water. Food so prepared then looks, smells and tastes fresh. Much of it is identical with that enjoyed by our boys who flew to the moon. It is not to be compared with the harsh "survival" hardtack and condensed stuff used in army emergencies. This new food is always appetizing.

We already have "meals on wheels" whereby hot dinners are distributed to elders, taken right to their homes. But of those 6,000,000 needy ones, fewer than 300,000 now receive those meals, and none at all is delivered on Saturdays and Sundays nor to isolated persons. Some churches have TLC (Tender Loving Care) programs whereby indigent elderly folk can get free meals in pleasant surroundings once a day. But many persons cannot get to those churches.

Newness, then. New trends, new techniques in national and personal health and in dedicated charity. A new life way for aging poor people; a new grandeur and hope. In short— humanitarian progress.

HELP FEED THOSE FRIENDS

This progress brings up another heartening trend among aging folk who are "well to do" and have time on their hands. A spreading custom is for *them* to take on nutrition programs for less fortunate elders.

That becomes a very soul-satisfying godly outreach. Not only do the financially-able ones deliver food to poor folk, they deliver fellowship and friendship and countless lesser helps. An outreach! A life sharing! Which, the authorities tell us, is a perfect hedge against mental illness and senility.

Many elderly-helping-the-elderly groups are popping up across the nation, expanding that TLC ideal. Very often a church or synagogue becomes the control center for such an activity.

In short—aren't old people wonderful?

"HOW WAS THAT AGAIN?"

One health warning can hardly be repeated too often: among the great tragedies of modern life is the new onslaught of deafness or partial deafness.

No human being was ever meant to lose his wonderfully acute hearing, and for millions of years relatively few people did lose it. But today's generation of aging persons—whoo! You have no idea how many millions of us are afflicted. But the *really* bad news is that the situation is certain to get worse. You who are now aged 35 or so—for heaven's sake, take heed. This new horror of partial and even total deafness on the American (and international) scene is due primarily to young people's obsession with amplified "musical" sounds, plus airplane and motorcycle roarings, and many other hour-to-hour wham-bangings in general. Thus in a very short time more than half our nation's citizens will have to face loss of hearing. A tragedy for sure.

Most of the trouble is due to nerve deafness, and there is no cure for it. The only preventive is—relative quiet. (My own relatives are *never* quiet! Especially my grandchildren! . . . Excuse me, please). We are all children of nature. We were first put into a Garden, remember, and expected to live there in quiet happiness. The only really loud, explosive noise in nature is a clap of thunder, and we experience that only a few times a year, hence our ears were designed to cope. They cannot cope with the daily, hourly, incessant crashings of what we call civilization. Ask any otologist.

I have already told you how difficult it is for people with good hearing to accept the annoyance caused them by people who are deaf or partially deaf. It is a strange psychological situation. You must all keep in mind that "hearing aids" positively do NOT restore your normal hearing. Every sound, through any hearing aid stuck into the ear or hanging around it or used in any manner, seems as if it were coming through a tin can cupped over your ear. That tinny, metallic effect virtually kills all music for you. Also, the aid loses many low-key voices, and is not selective in crowds of four or more people. With hearing aids, you are still unable to enjoy most lectures or other public speeches (with rare exceptions). So for heaven's sake protect your ears! Avoid explosive noises; gun shots, trip-hammers on pavements, closeups of jet airplane engines, outrageously loud "give" on hi-fi music in the home, anything similar. Or you will surely pay dearly for your negligence in later years, and even soon ones.

Another factor here is the cost. I have consulted electronics experts about this. They can manufacture all kinds of transistorized big gadgets using electricity and working miracles, for relatively little money nowadays. But hearing aids? Those tiny bits for your ear? You will pay from $400 to $1,500 for them as I write this, and the price is constantly rising. That much *each;* double it for both ears. Undoubtedly this is a ripoff, just as the outrageous price of an automobile is, and as the maddening bills from most hospitals are, the dishonesties of which are rationalized by blaming everything on "inflation." Phooey. It is such dishonest advantage taking that *encourages* inflation. But such is our vaunted capitalistic system, and it unquestionably is going to have to be reorganized. It is just such misuse of it that gives the contemptible communists material for propagandizing us. Sometimes we Americans and Canadians tend to dig our own graves.

If you seem to be a little "hard of hearing," then, go immediately to a competent otologist. That's an expert, a licensed physician specializing in ear problems. Do NOT go first to some hearing-aid store or salesman, do not order aids by mail until the otologist has examined you and given you his counsel. Ask your trusted family physician to recommend a reputable otologist. This is important for your hearing and your bank account.

At the very moment when I am writing this, my beloved wife has stuck her head in my door behind my back and said "I think it's going to snow."

I flipped the little switch that silences my typewriter, sat there a moment, thinking. This is June 4. Moreover, in our hometown it *never* snows. So—once more, for the millionth time at least, I had to turn around, look at her lips, and ask the age-old question used by us deefies—"How was that again?"

The sweet thing had said, "Why don't we go to the show?"

"Go; going. Snow; show. Sounds that seem much alike to people with hearing aids. We lose the *ing* syllables entirely. We lose the deep gutterals, the murmured tones.

When people enunciate perfectly, we hear everything clearly; but not one person in 50 does enunciate well. Therefore I (and all deefies) have a choice: 1) I can get mad. 2) I can wallow in self-pity. 3) I can be infinitely patient, get out of my chair, walk close, look the speaker right in the face, smile kindly, and say, "How was that again?"

MENTAL ILLNESS

In building a life way for the last quarter of the 20th century and adapting to ever-broadening phenomena and knowledge in all fields, we have to consider our minds. This is a *health* consideration, not a cultural one. It is an absolute imperative for each one of us.

On the American, Canadian and English scenes (and undoubtedly everywhere else) mental illness ranks Number One as a health problem. One out of every 12 Americans and Canadians who enter hospitals are there because of mental illness, and millions more ought to be there. Thus saith our experts. There is some evidence that the problem is slightly less in Canada, and there are small areas in the USA where there seems to be no mental illness at all. Even the expert psychiatrists wonder why. All in all, mental illness is a *major* consideration for each of us. Or—let me express it with a more upbeat tone: our mental *health* must be our major consideration, as we turn 40 or so birthdays and focus on upgrading the second half of our lives.

The aging ones past 40, perhaps not too surprisingly, are not as prone toward mental illness as are members of the stress ridden younger folk. Perhaps this is because we have acquired a bit more wisdom, have learned something of how to cope with life's vicissitudes. It was elderly Mrs. Verna Vicissitude, you know, who went to her doctor with her mental illness. She said to him, "I seem to be losing my memory, losing my mind. I mean, I forget everything. It is very disturbing.

Dr. Bill Zarhigh soft-pedaled. "There, there, I know what you mean. Memory loss is a real problem. But I will do everything I can to help you, so do not despair. Now, how long have you had this condition?''

Whereupon Verna looked blankly at him and said ''What condition?''

It tain't funny! In fact, I resent all the heartless comedians who make jokes on television and elsewhere about people who are mentally ill. Whenever opportunity arises, I tell them off. Jokes about the psychiatrist's couch are in exceedingly poor taste.

But our fictional Verna's condition is so common to ALL of us, even many under age 40, that it underscores a point that I want to make here, to wit: *lapses in memory do not necessarily connote mental illness.*

''I forget your face, but I remember your name.''

''I remember your name, but I forget your face.''

''Where DID I put my car keys? I must be getting old.''

You well know the pattern; the all-too-common bits of forgetfulness.

But few of them really amount to much. Most are just momentary annoyances, and they stem from the fact that your mind has been focused on other things, likely on matters that are much more important.

Latch onto that, and take comfort. Such forgetting is common to college kids and scientists and philosophers and all of us, because the mind tends to focus on importances and momentarily dismiss or ignore any onwonted distractions. That's good! That's where creativity develops.

Mental *illness* connotes a major loss of mental and emotional control, usually accompanied by disorientation and/or deep depression, unreasonable anxieties and fears, sleeplessness, nervousness, and in the extreme—violence.

Most of us, considering ourselves normal, feel that mental illness occurs only in *other* people. If this attitude focuses on one person (for instance your mate or other close one) and you keep seeing, thinking and saying how ''disturbed'' that one is—the chances are that YOU need to go to the psychiatrist! Remember that.

No no no, a thousand times no, do NOT trek down to some recommended "analyst" and spend a lot of money and time on him, just because you haven't been sleeping well lately, or have been having sex fantasies maybe, or your mate has been irritating you unduly, or some such. After all, you do have will power, and you can usually take charge of your thinking and set it to rights. So avoid the quacks. It has been stylish for active folk to "go to an analyst" in recent years. Also the social scene has been sullied by endless so-called "parlor" psychiatrists," meaning family members or friends who think they are somehow experts at psychology and are eager to tell you precisely what you should do. These too are quacks. Tell them to hush up and mind their own business. You can be mentally ill, and still have a great backlog of intelligent common sense.

If you are indeed suffering *persistent* delusions, depressions, aberrations or other mental phenomena which in your rational moments you know are abnormal, do quietly ask your family physician to recommend a competent psychiatrist or clinic, or perhaps a clinical psychologist. (Every psychiatrist is in some measure a psychologist; but every psychologist is not a psychiatrist. Very often, a psychologist is all that a disturbed person needs.) Sometimes just a quiet visit or two with your minister, your priest, your rabbi, will solve a personal problem for you; in fact this kind of service is a major part of our church leaders' godly outreach.

Now pause a moment here, take a deep breath and relax yourself. Because I have another shocker for you, one that is certain to haunt your mind for the remainder of your life:

One of America's most renowned psychiatrists, one who is highly honored, says that "Eighty percent of all the mental illness that comes before me could have been prevented, or could yet be cured, by *simple kindness!*"

What do you think of THAT? . . . Simple homespun kindness.

What a devastating commentary on our mores and manners, our habits and hangups! We who pose as good Christians or good Jews or other god-fearing persons.

YOUR BIORHYTHMS—WHATEVER *THEY* ARE

Do not feel embarrassed. I don't know what they are, either. "To the best of my knowledge and belief, at this point in time" (I am still aping the Watergators) I have no viable vibrations of memory which tell me that we raised any biorhythms at all on our farm and ranch when I was a boy in Texas. Perhaps the climate and the soil were not conducive to them there. *Biorhythms?* Even the governor of the state would have stared at you, bewildered, back there in 1912 or so.

But if you could have told the governor what is *now* known about biorhythms, he would surely have asked the Legislature for a big Committee and a big appropriation to propagate and improve them, Progress being the hallmark of Texans.

Why is it that some days you feel like you are on top of the world, and other days you feel like the world is on top of you?

You know very well that we all do go through such cycles. Okay, those cycles are called biorhythms. And a big part of that New Knowledge that I keep stressing, has been a better understanding of biorhythms and what we must do about them. Classify this as Good News.

Each one of us has three of them.

One is a 23-day physical cycle.

Another is a 28-day emotional cycle.

The third is a 33-day intellectual cycle.

In each one, we also have up periods and down periods. By knowing when you are "up" biorhythmically, you can put your ambitions and energies to much better use, you can achieve more, and feel like a million dollars at 20 percent interest. You are creative then.

The further Good News is—by knowing when you are "down" biorhythmically, you can give yourself a definite psychological shot in the arm, a personality pickup. You can sit at your own steering wheel; can, literally, guide yourself through old age.

No no, this is not hocus-pocus. Didn't I warn you not to let yourself become an old fuddy-duddy with a closed mind? So keep you mental doors open here. Knowledge of biorhythms dates back at least to the Victorian Era, but little was done about educating the masses of us to them until 1970 or so. Today we know that they begin in every person at the very moment of birth, and stay with us for life.

That's all I shall tell you about them, because that's all I know about them, and because I would need all of this book to help you explore them further. But I urge you to start reading, talking, sharing and learning how control of biorhythms can upgrade your total physical, emotional and intellectual health. Isn't that an intriguing thought? New knowledge, for a new life way, in a creative endeavor that can work wonders for all concerned.

In short, we—YOU!—of the alert ''now'' people at middle age or so, must take a wholly new approach to maintaining good health for yourself and your loved ones. The homemade sulphur-and-molasses spring tonic era is long, long gone.

9

What About
Your Sexual "Freedom?"

Continuing your physical, mental and emotional health program of adapting to newness, developing new attitudes in pursuit of happiness and general life success, you must face up to this:

> *Man's and woman's abiding "dream" is for*
> *sexual compatibility between man and wife.*

If he/she have that subtle, sacred, supremely satisfying relationship, it matters not whether they reside in a castle or a cave.

Now do not frown! Do not shrug and turn away.

This will be no sermon, no trite lecture replete with clichés. But the new "modern" attitude toward mating in our nation (and other nations as well) absolutely demands careful re-inspection to see if it is valid.

In point of fact, that attitude has two opposing aspects:

1. The feeling (to which I heartily subscribe) that far too many people age 15 to 90 are either occupied or preoccupied with sex too much of the time.

2. The feeling that this is a *now* generation, living in an enlightened era in which old moralistic standards are fuddy-duddy amusing, and should be cast aside in favor of unrestricted sexual "freedom," even if that involves homosexuality and other aberrations.

IT STARTS EARLY

As you well know, we do not wait until middle age for that dream of compatibility to begin. I recall my own personal deep yearning for a perfect sweetheart-wife relationship. It began when I was aged 10. I awoke one night, horrified. I had dreamed of a girl named Margaret Louise. At school, she had done no more than smile at me, bite a cookie in half and give me the other half. Just that triviality triggered something in my body chemistry, my psyche, or whatever. My lurid, technicolored, wonderful dream that night was unforgettable—but it also was a wet one.

Nobody had prepared me for that. In my ranch-farm milieu I had learned—from observing our horses, cows, hogs, chickens and dogs—that sexual union was necessary for the preservation of those species. From that I had wisely deduced what were and still are called the human "facts of life," meaning life's creation. That knowledge was scientifically verified by snickering comments, actions an innuendoes from older boys; one does learn from one's contemporaries.

Most men of my age had that experience in youth, back yonder when both we and the century were young. Girls were less fortunate; most grew into adulthood totally ignorant. "Sex"? The word was not even in the common language then; merely to utter it would have been a shame and a sin. Married women got themselves into "a family way," though God only knows how. One older friend of mine died recently; and shortly before, he said that he had fathered 12 children, but never once in all his life had he seen his wife naked between the ankles and the neck. Well, poor man; he never knew what he missed. My own brother's bride, a university graduate and schoolteacher mind you, thought that babies were born through the navel, and had no idea at all as to what started them until she married. That was in the enlightened year of 1916. Parents in general rarely dished out any formal sex education, and our schools—never. At my own age 12, the Grand Crush was with a lovely child named Eddie, for Edwina. At 15-plus, she gave way to a high school sophomore named Sarah—and *her* I still remember with complete vividness. She and I definitely planned to elope and live happily ever after. That avowal was in April, and we meant everything we said to one another, because young-adult maturity was dawning then.

By September, circumstance, not choice, had separated us. Inevitably we forgot each other, outwardly. But 41 years later I went back to that smallish East Texas town because it was throwing a grand celebration honoring me for having written a prize winning Literary Award Novel with the town as its setting (Title : *The Golden Chair*). The entire country closed all schools and business houses for a day, staged a mile-long parade with floats depicting scenes from the book, held speeches in Town Square and a huge banquet that night, with me signing hundreds of books in front of a sidewalk store; "the biggest book review in history," it was called, with some accuracy. And at the banquet, who came smiling up to me but—Sarah.

No outcry. No quick hug or kiss. No demonstrativeness at all. We just stared at each other in mutual recognition for a moment. Then she spoke softly—"We might have made a go of it, mightn't we?"

Ah, yes. We might have at that. By then, she was long married to the town bottler of soda pop, had two sons, and a happy life. In 1976 I visited her grave; she had died of cancer.

Meanwhile, of course, my own deeply dedicated love had shifted, in college, to the campus beauty, Adele. As I write this, she is about 30 feet from me, baking a cake. We have three daughters, eight grandchildren, 52 years of marriage—and get this—a private memory of complete sexual compatibility.

Few old couples can say that.

Fewer still, among younger couples, can claim complete sexual compatibility. Too many millions of them "rat" on one another; cheat, sneak off and go to bed with other people.

Saying all this, of course, makes me much holier-than-thou. And I do indeed take a quiet pride in having been loyal to my wife. If this confession makes me a jerk in your estimation—then get lost; you and I are not on the same wave length at all. My grand overall point here is—*honor among high-level Americans has not become outmoded or disappeared!* This applies to the quietly wonderful folk in all faiths, all colors, all occupations and locations.

It does *not* apply to the "modern" millions who have opted for sexual promiscuity. This group—say the physicians, the clergymen, the psychiatrists, the counselors, even the judges and police—have inescapably combined sexual promiscuity with anxiety.

THE PEAK OF FEAR

Those authorities (and my own observation; likely yours too) also say that the anxiety part of it peaks when the people are about age 40. That's the moment when you *should* be reaching the first truly high level of relaxed maturity and happiness in life. Instead, if you are a "sex freedom" activist, suddenly here it dawns on you that—good heavens—I have made a fool of myself; grandmother was right after all.

So—from now on out, what are you going to do about that?

Having shacked up with assorted loose women of negligible morals, or having been a super-pseudo-sophisticated swinging "single" who took any attractive feminine meat wherever you found it, married or not, what are you going to do *now,* sir? Go on as before? Change? Reform?

The same questions are addressed to you, madam, or miss; or forsooth, Ms—whatever that is. Now that the bloom of youth is off your face, replaced by the hard look, the cynical attitude, the painted-on smile, the crow's feet, the touched-up graying hair—what of your own future?

At age about 40, these questions for both sexes are inescapable. The authorities on aging say that they rank first in your conscience and consciousness. If your second 40 years are to offer any hope of being the best part of your life, those questions have to be answered with deep, introspective analysis and intelligent thinking. You cannot shrug them off, and coast. You cannot drown them in alcohol. You cannot erase them with nicotine or even with heroin. Absolutely you cannot evade the questions. If you try forcing yourself to ignore them, very soon you will truly be an "old and beaten" man or woman, though chronologically still youngish.

The major factor at this point in your life is the lurking power of that intangible we call Conscience.

You may outwardly flaunt the conventions. You may say that virginity before marriage is Victorian and outmoded. You may even say that loyalty to just one mate *after* marriage is Puritanical, is stupid, is unhealthy.

But that kind of thinking and arguing is pure rationalization. It is a psychic straining. Because, in point of fact, even if you do join that clan of swinging "modern" thinkers, the deep psychological studies reveal that *you are not sure of yourself.* In the affluent, materialistic, self-pampering society you have jauntily joined the parade. Now, suddenly, your feet are tired; as is your heart.

The human conscience has not been expunged from the human race. It still is the divine spark; the one thing that separates man from the animals.

"Thou shalt not commit adultery" is still etched on the stone tablet that figuratively adorns your bedroom. That Commandment is an emphatic law. It has not been declared unconstitutional by either state or church. It is still very much a Force.

NO ESCAPE IS POSSIBLE

Psychiatrists and psychologists well know how powerful that Commandment is in the human conscience and consciousness. Some innate awareness, some instinctive or intuitive knowledge tells you that illicit sex is wrong, wrong, wrong.

You may try hard to deny that, may smirk and grimace and strive loftily to ridicule the thought; or you may simply be a sheep and trot along with The Crowd, determined to do what you think is the "in" thing.

But it won't jell. In the deep recesses of your heart where you always hide the things of which you are ashamed—there it is, still nagging you. In your private moments alone—say at 3 a.m. in a night of restlessness—you *know!* Tomorrow you may put on a bold front again, denying. But secretly you still *know.* What you have done, and still are doing, is psychologically wrong and dangerous, it is spiritual evasion, it is poking your head into the sand, and your awareness can never be expelled by you alone. Ask the psychiatrists, the vaunted "analysts" who (for fat fees) listen to the outpourings of the ultra-sophisticated and overly publicized stars of stage, television, motion pictures and sports. What it all adds up to—like it or not—is that *no human being who sins can escape the wrath of God!* Never!

TELL ALL. *ALL!*

It is true that redemption of the human soul can come then, but it is proportionately harder. Even if you are already past age 50 or 60 or 70 and have that lost-soul feeling, that haunting inner awareness of a misled, mistaken life, past and present, then go at once to your minister, priest or rabbi, and Tell All. Tell Everything.

Pour it all out. Empty the garbage container. Drain the reservoir of shame. This is therapeutic cleansing; it can be very healing, comforting, reassuring. Done *sincerely,* mind you, it becomes your plea for divine forgiveness as well as for self-forgiveness. About which, God has said, *"Ask, and ye shall receive."* Which is the most comforting of all promises, no matter what age we may be.

But be warned—you cannot cheat on that!

You dare not to try to take unfair advantage. It will require some suffering; especially mental anguish. A few nominal Catholics, mistaking their own church doctrine, hold that they can raise all the hell they want to during the week, then go to confession on Sunday and get absolution. No such! This is NOT true Catholic doctrine. Certainly it is not Protestant nor Jewish doctrine. You simply can never be a selfish jerk in *any* religious culture, then grinningly buy your way out of guilt and responsibility. Common sense should tell you that. But common sense is a woefully uncommon commodity. Positively, dearly beloveds, you can never, never, flaunt all sexual restrictions and cater only to momentary carnal desire.

THE DECENT SET

It is a strange, strange fact that in this enlightened era even millions of virtuous people middle-aged and older do not "understand" the rather simple facts about sex.

"Is three times a week too much?" they ask their physicians and other counsellors, rather wistfully.

It is.

The best concensus-advice that I can find for you is—sexual intercourse should be restricted to something like once every week or 10 days, perhaps with occasional exceptions.

Intercourse is a tremendous physical and psychic binge any time. It is not a mere half hour or half minute of physical union with sundry motions and pantings and exclamations and orgasms and such, it is also a deep straining and draining of the inner forces, both physical and emotional. Thus you must not allow yourself to become obsessed with sex, as many do. Every night? You are begging for trouble! You are opening the gate for critical psychic fatigue; which is the worst kind. You will soon be a jaded old gent or gal, even if you are barely into your twenties, or indeed if you are a teenager with great initial virility.

Just how long do you think the prostitutes last? A high school girl becomes promiscuous. She continues that through college. At that age she is nubile, alluring, sassy and cute and pink and pretty with maximum come-on. Females of her type make Big Money; some earn $100 or up to $500 a night, especially the "high class" Call Girls, which often includes luscious young matrons.

Then around age 28 to 30—BLOOP! The balloon bursts.

Nobody "calls" them anymore; no rich executive, ratting on his wife when he goes off to a distant convention or equal, hires a hotel pimp to put him in touch with the Marguerite with whom he "made love" (a common but ridiculous euphemism; you don't make love in such instances, you make *lust*) so illicitly on former trips. She is now—jaded? Washed up? Yes! Her act in bed becomes forced, mechanical, uninspired. She is hard bodied and hardhearted, working only for money, and in desperation at that, straining to hold onto what she thinks of as her youth, beauty and charm.

The life range of a whore (which is what all such are, of course, even the "high class" girls) averages little more than 10 years. She becomes worn out, her bloom lost, her sex appeal negligible except to very low type males who are as bad off as she. No wonder the suicide rate among such people is tragically high.

"Happiness?" The word never really registers for them. Such folk do not *live* at all, they merely exist. Their minds have been so ossified, so grooved, that they are totally incapable of getting away from their "professions." So for escape they resort to alcohol and harsher drugs, then to crime in order to get money to get the drugs. They become humanity's outcasts. And—heaven help us—most such still are not yet 40 years of age.

All that has been true since long before Cleopatra seduced that young chap on her Nilean barge. It is more true today than ever, right here in Los Angeles and Reno and Denver and New Orleans and Miami and New York and Chicago and Toronto and Victoria and around the globe. This, dearly beloveds, is the current Great Sociological Tragedy of the human race; the misuse of sex.

YOU TOO, MISTER

Now, sir, everything said above—*applies to you as well!*

The male human being has no superiority, no immunity from moral squalor and wretchedness.

The male of whatever age who calls the Call Girl, or who picks up the garish barfly, or who responds to the street walker, or who seduces the sweet neighbor girl, positively is as much a prostitute, a whore, as is the female involved, and generally is even more contemptible. He cannot deny his stupidity or guilt, ever. It is not *her* fault, not *his* fault, it is THEIR fault. The blame is equal.

Many males in their conceit and fatuous ignorance will deny this. They are wrong; and in their secret inner moments they know it. This awareness kills them. Kills their spirits, sears their souls. Thus they rapidly become frantic, soured, anxiety ridden, embittered, mean. They suffer all manner of physical ills in addition to such routine infections as gonorrhea and syphilis. Early heart attacks, for instance; many a thousand man has died while straining for his orgasm on top of a woman—ask any physician. Then there are strokes. Acute digestive troubles, emotionally induced. Mental aberrations beyond all reckoning. And yes, suicides.

Proof of this horror is best found in that cesspool area generally tagged "Las Vegas" but meaning all of Nevada. (Forgive me, you high class people in that state. But that's the way the rest of the nation sees you). The suicide rate in Nevada is appalling—though generally it is unpublicized, hushed up; far and away the biggest percentage in the nation. This is due partly to money losses in gambling, which are astronomical: But the main cause of such desperation, the authorities reveal, is general moral decline, starting with or ending with divorce, and generally the collecting there of so many "promiscuous" and predatory females and males, the don't-care types, the defiant jet-set self-pampering and women who for a few years fancy themselves immune to evil influences and somehow superior to humble God-fearing folk.

That Las Vegas syndrome, that fallacious worship of sexual "freedom" which really means whoring promiscuity, can be found in areas of other states, of course. The big point here is—repeat—*does it apply to you?* wherever you live?

Does it?

Honestly now, *does it?* Whoever you are, wherever you are,

whatever your sex, age or environment—does it?

Can you ignore the religious undergirding of America? "Oh come off of it!" you may scoff. "Nobody takes religion seriously anymore, nobody goes to church nowadays. This is not the year 1900."

Hoo boy, how wrong can you be! In 1978 there were 250 million *more* Christians in the world than in 1970—imagine! Because of population shifts, which are prodigious, *some* churches have declined in membership, a few have closed down. But many more new ones have been launched, many hundreds of thousands of converts to Christianity alone. I am an usher in a big church. Each Sunday we pack the sanctuary full, all main-floor pews, two transcepts, two balconies. Fifteen minutes from my home, a genius-preacher named Bob Schuller is constructing the largest, costliest, most impressive cathedral ever known on this earth—a breathtaking "Crystal Cathedral" with an initial cost of 15 million dollars, an all-glass structure dedicated to Christ. "Nobody goes to church anymore?" Don't be stupid, you have simply been wearing dark glasses, probably inside dark cocktail lounges and bars. Get out of there and learn what is *really* going on in this grand American world.

SOME TONES ARE GRAY

We do not quite paint the social and moral picture all black or white. Definitely there are gray tones. In millions of the "modern" loose-living adults there comes a sudden psychological shock wave, resulting in deep turmoil. These heartsick people, straining for relief, confess their sexual sins to their spouses and plea for forgiveness.

But instead of bringing relief, the self-condemnation and self-pity all too often simply burden the offender with guilt that should have been borne forever, alone. In other words, it is not always imperative that either mate tell the other one "everything."

If you have a lingering shame and truly want to reform— say the very best authorities—quietly make your sincere confession to a trained minister, priest or rabbi, then calmly, determinedly go forth toward new and brighter horizons, making whatever tactful restitution you can, but seeking no sympathy and nursing no self-abasement or shame.

I myself am not a clergyman. Definitely I cannot "run your life" for you, cannot coerce or force you in any manner whatsoever. My position is simply that of a trained reporter and research man, with a talented editor who forces me to sift out the absolute facts for you and suggest how you may use them.

I am not contemptuous of you, either; not at all. I wish you well. I encourage you—no matter what your age or present condition—to cling fast to that grandest of all grand concepts, hope. By trying hard to adapt to newness and reality, making every effort toward upgrading the remaining part of your life, you have absolutely nothing to lose.

You take it from here.

TEN SURE WAYS TO BLIGHT YOUR TROTH (A RECAPITULATION)

The middle-age of 35 to 45 or so is a major checkpoint in marriage. It is here that, all too often, divorce suddenly looms as attractive, a solution to all your marital woes. In truth, though, divorce *any* time is a proclamation of failure, of personal inadequacy in choosing a mate and developing a happy married life. The national rush into divorce in recent years has been a tragic disillusionment for millions who rather flippantly or impulsively went into it. These learn the hard way that divorce invariably creates more problems than it solves, even those that are called "friendly" or "compatible" or some such nonsense. Professional counselling has become big business, with its promise to help the separated or divorced woman "find herself," or the man "discover his true destiny." The cost of this runs around $100 per hour, and most of it is merely vague poppycock, catering to conceit, false pride and self-pity. True, earnest counsellors do sometimes offer good advice; and serve as a needed listener to the distressed one's woes. But the interest is completely impersonal, with little or no spiritual motivation.

If you have a grain of intelligence, you will recognize that *any* marriage is a tenderling, a hot-house flower. It cannot stand much "cold," and will wilt with equal quickness under too much "heat" whether psychic or sexual. Any marriage that is thus left unguarded, uncultivated, is likely to wither and die. Any man or woman who lets the marriage wither or dwindle, is plunging toward despair.

Those, however, are desperately true generalities only. So now let us tighten down some specifics. There are at least ten of them which we can list as sure ways to blight your troth, whether it began yesterday or many years ago. Inspect them carefully, then decide which ones apply in your marriage, and what must be done about them.

1. Resist Change.

Change in your life-style is inevitable. Then why in heaven's name do you resist it? Having been a "single," *of course* you must change when you marry. You can no longer demand all your old patterns and standards of living—unless you really want to blight your marriage. Absolutely, the woman *must* leave her parents, both physically and psychologically. Nor can the man cling mentally to his old home. You who are now middle-aged or more, doubtless have come to realize all this.

But have you adapted to other newness in life? Are you "tough," inflexible in opinions, hard-boiled in attitudes toward the government, the neighbors, the boss, the employees, the children? Do you demand the same general home routine always? The same types of clothing, vacation, music, books, "sameness" at every turn?

Do you "hate" the President? The governor, mayor, boss, anybody at all who might not have pleased you at some point? We all have momentary "hatreds." Can you change yours, to "weave with the times" in achieving intellectual progress?

2. Buy, Buy, Buy.

"Buy" quickly becomes synonymous with "blight." Ask any banker. No matter how long you have been married, it is astounding how *little* you really need in order to be happy together. Newlyweds' most common mistake is installment buying, straining for "things." Middle age has the problem of keeping up with the Joneses; self-pampering with too many luxuries. "Status," forsooth! Straining for social position and prestige, feeding the joint egos, with costly clothing, cars and other status symbols, is a major marriage blight.

3. Let Recreation Wreck Creation.

Millions of couples are shallow enough in their thinking to approach marriage as they would a senior prom; gaiety and dancing and self-indulgences, but little else. And so the divorce rate soars. The disillusionment strikes hardest at middle age. Play alone is soul stifling; you have to *work* your way through marriage. Happy marriage is high-level creativity; too much "recreation" or play wrecks it.

4. Encourage Sexual Debauchery.

You have already been warned about that. It can blight any troth, and destroy any marriage. Illicit sex—at any age from 10 to 100—violates all moral law and the law of the land; and common sense. It quickly kills every golden dream. It strikes often among aging folk who think they are "tired of" their mates, or want to boost their egos with "affairs" outside of marriage.

5. Ignore Possible Mental Illness.

This too has already been discussed here. But review it, if you want your "troth" to stay unblighted. Knowledge of mental illness is the best preventive. Remember the famed psychiatrist's warning: "Eighty percent of all the mental illness that appears before me could have been prevented, or could yet be cured, by *simple kindness.*" Which is just another way of saying that tenderness is the one indispensable emotion. Tenderness! . . . Understand?

6. Neglect a Wholesome Sense Of Humor.

Chapter 5 of this book discusses the importance of humor in detail. Go back to it, for a review. The sum of it is—a wholesome sense of humor is equal in value to a wholesome sense of morals, because one balances the other. This is an extremely important concept; and sadly, it is generally ignored.

7. Show No Appreciation.

Literally, we live to be loved; to be admired and appreciated. The other party in any troth cannot assume your love and appreciation, *you must express it.* "They do not love," Shakespeare warned us, "who do not *show* their love." It must never be taken for granted. The husband is most often at fault in this, notably the one at middle age and older. "She knows I love her," he will grouse, if pressed about it. "Why do I have to be mushy?" She would be better off without you around! Because she could then at least fanticize your happy nature. Appreciation is synonymous with sincerity. It is not merely speaking to, it is doing for, sharing.

Are you intelligent enough to grasp the profound truth of that? If you aren't—your marriage is doomed.

8. Inept Communication.

Go back and re-study Chapter 4. Then etch it on your aging brain that not only what you say to your mate, but how you say it, are of extreme importance, forever. Best way to blight a troth is to become surly, critical, short-tempered, demanding, selfish, "hurt" or touchy. This leads to stupid bickering. Remember those truths, discussed above, about tenderness and good humor.

9. Coast.

Do you *really* want to blight your troth, your marriage? Then cease pedaling. Coast! Drift along. Make no effort. Assume that the problem is entirely your mate's.

And prepare for a big bustup soon. It is inevitable.

10. Repress Your Altruism.

If you don't know what altruism is, you are already in trouble. Altruism is simply an unselfish concern for the welfare of others. It is the opposite of selfishness. It starts with some definite give ups.

It has nothing to do with obnoxious "do-goodism," but is a genuine inner spiritual outreach. No individual, no couple, no club or other group, ever *ever* achieved any real happiness or "success" without altruism.

Does that tell you something, dearly beloveds?

10

Your Rapport With Youth

Whether we like it or not—and to be honest about it, very often we don't—we old heads aged 35 to 95 have to live with children.

I know, I know—they are "sweet" and lovable and enlivening and inevitable and all that; don't get your hackles up. But sentimentality about them fluctuates, you know. You might as well be honest about it; sometimes kids overwhelm even you.

So there is no need for any of us to be mushy-nice about children, any more than there is a need to be cruel to them. We DO love them. In fact we also envy them, and wish we could stay childlike forever. The Bible itself suggests that we must do just that. However—in terms of mentality and emotions, actions and reactions, we and they are light-years apart.

It has been that way since the beginning of time. I suspect that maybe it was a deliberate arrangement, by a divine providence that wanted to teach *both* factions of us how to handle that concept which—as I have repeatedly told you now—is the main theme of this book—adaptability. Kids do have to adapt to us who are twice their height and weight and more. And certain it is an exercise in adapting whenever Mom and Pop strive to get along pleasantly with Junior and Sister.

"Rapport" today is an overworked word. Yet we must use it because there is no real substitute or synonym. It translates to mean getting along with each other, happily, successfully, for all parties concerned. It connotes more than mere "understanding," it holds the added grandeur of putting up with; which is to say—tolerance.

If you tolerate the kids, they will tolerate you.

True, true, you adults have Responsibility here. But not all of it! They owe you something, too. In family yak-sessions, powwows, conferences, this point should be made very clear. Surprisingly, the youngsters often grasp it more quickly than the adults do.

"My Mom has 'sponser billeries,' " I recall overhearing one little sugar-pie person tell her playmates. "She has to love my Daddy at night and I can't sleep in bed with them."

Well all right! Facts are facts, and she was latching onto a few of them. Mom explained to this little daughter that some day she too would have a husband-daddy-man and have to sleep with him while *her* children stayed in their own rooms and beds. The message was accepted.

Youngsters *want* to assume Responsibilities—"sponser billeries"—want to do their share. This is a deep-felt yearning in them, in their eagerness to grow up and Be Somebody, be adult. Wherefore if you, Mom and Pop, make any kind of gentle effort at all, you can enjoy perfect rapport with Junior and Sister who are under age 12, also with that second magnificent category of braintrusters, the teenagers, now generally referred to as "young adults."

YOU DON'T NEED A BOOK

We could write a book about all this. As a matter of fact, at least 500 different books must already have been published on how to have perfect rapport with children, and all such.

But you don't need a book.

We can make one exception to that statement—you do need *The* Book; the one that guides almost all of America and humanity elsewhere, in how to have a successful life. For many years it has been the world's best-seller, by more than 10 to one over any other. If you don't know the title of that book here at your age, you really *are* in trouble.

But lesser authors have come out with books, and some of them do offer sound counsel, and most of it is based on the common sense that you probably already possess. In my research for this chapter of this book, I asked several experts about all that.

"Just tell your readers to ignore all complicated instructions," those good people advised me, "and begin applying their own sound instincts. That's what common sense is. You do this by the technique of *reversal*. Let each parent or guardian say to himself/herself, 'What would I want from my parents if I were my children's age? And what could I give them, in turn?' Do this thinking first, in private, then with your mate in private conversation. Do not try to be a parlor psychiatrist, 'analyzing' any young boy or girl. Instead, just 'talk your nerves down,' as we say. Deliberately create mental and emotional relaxation with regard to your children. Drop any air of authoritarianism, any firm-lipped bossiness, all accusations and glarings and 'lecturing.'

"Instead, astonish them. Display a loving smile and say, 'Hey, let's go to a movie together tonight (or play games together at home, or similar). Okay? Suggest a skating party, a swim in lake or sea or pool, a backpacking trip, a set of tennis, anything at all that means togetherness. Come off your high horse, Pop and Mom; get down there with the juvenile minds. They can't come to yours, but you can come to their level. And that is the beginning of ideal rapport. But you the parent have to initiate it, because you have the mental maturity to do so and so often the youth doesn't. The youth may try; and if this happens, encourage it. But so often a youth acts, sullen, defiant, 'mixed up,' even while altogether hungry for what you have to give."

It is impossible for most children to think like adults. How could they, when they are not your age? But it is entirely possible for you to think like children, because you *have* been there.

The *mood* for building rapport absolutely must be given priority consideration by you and your mate. It must be casual, relaxed, calm, unhurried, soft-spoken, and above all—good humored. No "duty" stuff here. No direct or even veiled reference to "your responsibilities to us" or any such lecture tone. Love? Yes, of course. Just do not be mushy-gushy with it; be gentle, subtle. Assess no blame. Make no comparisons with yourself when *you* were young, except perhaps in fun. Do indicate that you are aware of the child's needs, and are anxious to help. Not punish, help.

Keep up this policy for a few days or until it becomes habitual. The results will be absolutely astounding. High old laughing happiness will reign in the household. I recall when the O'Reilly parents had several guests in for buffet dinner, to see their new home. Young daughter Erin and her father were showing one group around, when a man asked Erin, "Does your father have a den?" Erin replied, straight-faced but eyes sparkling, "Oh no sir. Daddy just growls all over the house." Then ran! With Pop pursuing her in mock anger. That's rapport!

Yes, do some "teaching." But be very sure it is gentle and kind, the put-down or critical type, never accusatory or belittling. As Erin's father had, encourage them to tease you in turn. Crack jokes at and with each other. Build that subtlety of happy-go-lucky atmosphere which is shown in laughter and singing and romping, along with some moments of hugging and showing the tender touch.

Rapport with youth? Heavens, it will grow like a runaway vine, the one that Jack the Giant Killer climbed! You have only to plant the seed.

HOW TO COPE WITH GRANDCHILDREN

The trouble with children is that *they* grow up and have children!

Thus it is that many a million bouncy, very young man under age 40 has suddenly and devastatingly been faced with the fact that he is a grandpappy. In which case you are likely to hear his howlings from Key West to Prudhoe Bay. They may be howling of pride, yes; but invariably there also is an undercurrent of anxiety. *Me*, a grandfather at age 38? *Me?* He can't believe it. He fancied himself still virtually a collegian, still holding youth's rah-rah attitudes.

Research shows that among women the young-grandmother trauma is even worse. NO woman is ever going to get old, you know. Never! And only old people are grandparents—aren't they? Very often the youngish grandmom, discovering a pregnant daughter or daughter-in-law, bursts into tears. Self-pity, of course; vanity. Just like the man's.

Such middle-agers are immature minded. We laugh at them, when we ought really to pity them. Sometimes we can help them, by making them convert apprehension into pride. Pride in being a GRAND! Then we must help them build a new sort of pride in getting old itself. Because any grandparent *is* getting old, you know. Let nobody try to sweet-talk you to the contrary, even if—as frequently happens—you become a grandparent before age 35.

I have to ask you for the umpteenth time—*what's wrong with getting old?* (Especially when you consider the alternative!) I have dinged at you *ad nauseam* about having to adapt to changing situations. So okay, here is another one; and becoming a grandparent can be made the happiest change of all. Generally, YOU are the one who has to make it so.

You have a choice. You can be a self-centered narcissistic old weakling, or you can truly become a new Force, showing emotional and spiritual strength. Which is about as trite-and-corny a statement as I could possibly make, but also happens to be inescapably true. It is "new" with every generation of middle-agers; and has been so since Adam and Eve beheld with astonishment their own first grandchild.

Grandparenthood is not a disaster!

It is a privilege; a promise, a new inspiration and opportunity for life enrichment, as the ancient clichés keep telling us. So why can't you believe them? Why must you be apprehensive, worrying, shedding tears? Certainly you are getting old. But what of it? There is a rightness about grandparent-hood. Trying to fight it, ignoring it, is unthinkable.

Grandparenthood can never just be taken for granted. Something must be *done* about it. Something, though we are never sure just what. So start by thinking a little; you know— thinking? To oneself? Using the brain? A too-little-used process nowadays! But you can do it. Maybe you could start by projecting yourself back into the Garden.

"Whatever are we gonna *do*, Adam?" the first grandma must have exclaimed. "Our boy Abel has a son."

"We are gonna love it and help bring it up properly, that's what."

I can't be sure Adam said that—I wasn't there at the time. But I hope he did. (And never mind about what girl Abel married in the first place! That's God's business, not yours or mine.)

I also hope that what Adam replied is approximately what you say when your grandbaby is born. You are going to love it, and be very proud of it, and make little jokes about its favoring your side of the family, and help your kids rear (not "raise," that's for livestock) it properly and help it become a fine upstanding citizen. Which brings up an immediate, potent question—how?

THE TRULY GRAND GRANDPARENTS

You'd think everybody would know, wouldn't you? You bring up a grandchild just like you bring up a child. Don't you?

No, you don't.

The new second-generation weeling is in a different world from the one its Mom and Pop entered. This has always been true. But how very weird were the beliefs and customs of our immediate yesteryears! I think back to my older brother Grady Arnold. He became a hotshot physician in a smallish Texas town, and frequently was called to some very rural home to help a baby into the world, and he always had problems there.

For instance, in that era and locale, it was standard practice to give the newborn baby a sliver of raw, fat bacon to suck, immediately after its birth. This was held to be not only nourishing, it was a symbol of love; the baby needed to eat, and feeding it was showing love because mama's milk would not "come in" for maybe 24 hours or more. Grady had a hard time correcting that folk custom. In fact he had a hard time before the delivery. The father threatened to shoot him if he looked at the naked wife lying there in childbirth pains. Before the muzzle of a shotgun, Dr. Arnold was expected to deliver that baby solely by feeling under a protective sheet. Grady got mad that day, stood up, challenged the young father, took the gun away from him and locked him out of the room. But the grandmother stayed and prayed while Grady delivered a squalling grandson with as much clinical cleanliness as conditions would permit. That baby, I happen to know, is a respected farmer in Rusk County, Texas, today.

One of my father's Negroes—we called them "ours" not from any hint of slavery, but because they lived on our acreage and we loved them and they loved us and we all helped one another—was a tall healthy housewife aged about 24 years. (And if you think this report sounds "racist," dear reader, you are wrong, this is accurate folk history). She was in a crew of cotton pickers one September day. As a 14-year-old son of the boss, I was the cotton weigher. At mid-morning weighing, neither Melissa Nichols nor her mother showed up with the usual sacks full of cotton to be weighed, though I knew both had been present. But at noon, Melissa did show up, a big happy smile beaming, her cotton sack full.

"Had me a new baby this morning," she told us all there, with obvious pride.

Another woman spoke out. "Me, I'm its grandmother. It look just like me!" Pride! Happiness!

Melissa had left the cotton rows about 9:30 a.m., gone into the shade of some hickory trees, laid down on cool soft grass, and borned herself a manchild. Wouldn't even let her mama help. Then after resting a bit, had gone back to picking cotton, and thought nothing of it. Routine. Common among many folk, both white and black, in that milieu. Expected of them. Today, *that* baby is a happy healthy farmer in that same country. Its grandmomma loved it, away back yonder in 1914. The black grandmomma brought it to our home to show it off to my mother and sister, who "made over" it with heartfelt lovings and chatter, and pitched in to help make it a layette. My father gave it a five-dollar bill at birth. The black mother had oodles of rich tittie milk—we called it that. So, when my brother's wife Norma had a baby real soon, papa would put his white granddaughter on a pillow between him and his saddle horn, and disappear for maybe half a day, overseeing the work on ranch and farm. When his white grandbaby needed attention, he rode by the home of the black Nichols family, handed his granddaughter to Melissa, who proudly changed it, cuddled it, fed it from her ample breasts, sang to it, rocked it, handed it back to "Mr. Will" Arnold, my dad. Papa would give Melissa a dollar for that; a shiny silver dollar.

Those were great times!

Halcyon days of yore. Back in the Stone Age, when I was a boy.

But the "moral" they point up is still valid—isn't it? Must I spell it out for you? Surely you see the undercurrents; of love and trust and sharing; of how grandparenthood should be approached, even now. Not with the same mechanics, no, but with the same spirit.

True, all of that is far behind us, and the grandmother of the late 20th century has an altogether different role because so many new customs have come into vogue. From this— you parents must learn that many of the customs of that era must give way to newness in *your* time. You do not have the same responsibilities that my parents had. STAY SOMEWHAT ALOOF.

Except in emergencies, today's grandparents must develop a policy of detachment. Every psychologist and family-life counsellor advises—do not poke in too far. Within reason, let the new parents alone, let them "run things" their way. They are likely to be smarter than you are, grandmom and grandpop. So you just wait to be *invited* into the affairs of the newborn child.

Even then, play it cool, as the teenagers say. If your direct advice is sought, say to the mother or father, "Why I wouldn't really want to answer that, darling. But I am sure your own instincts will guide you properly. You had a good rearing and schooling, you have a fine obstetrician and pediatrician. It would be presumptuous of us grandparents to try to run things now."

Is the point clear, old dears?

That way, you endear yourselves to the new parents. So unless there is critical illness or other need, *let the young parents direct and control the new baby's life,* while you two oldsters look benevolently on. Very quickly, Baby will develop a personality in his/her own right; will hold out little arms, look up at you and smile.

Oh boy! That does it. Sound the trumpets, beat the drums! No greater pleasure can come to the old ones than when the new grandbaby becomes Aware. A kind of divine spark is ignited; maybe it *is* divine; maybe it is electrical— we were exploring electricity in earlier chapters here, remember. No matter; whatever it is, the new rapport with the new human being, is utter happiness for all three concerned. Make the most of it.

11

"But I Just Want To Sit Down
And Do Nothing—

because I have worked hard all my life, and I have earned the
right to rest.''

Ah ha! So *that's* the dream you have bought!

It is in fact a typical theme-dream of millions who look
forward to ''retirement.''

It is the lush green grass on the Other Side Of The Fence—
the fence being, generally, age 65, but more recently 70 by
law, although it often is near age 40. Surely since Adam first
spoke them—if he did, and he probably did, having goofed
it and gotten booted out of the Garden—those words have
been spouted 77 hundred trillion times. Or more.

WISHFUL WISH

Okay okay, my old friend Aloysius McNamara said those
words, and in a measure they were correct. He *had* worked
hard all his life, he *had* earned the right to rest. I saw eye-to-
eye with him. I agreed with him completely. Good old pal
Wish McNamara; we had much in common.

Including short-sightedness, lamebrains!

I am a shanty Irishman myself, you know—have I
explained that? I do tend to forget, some. Anyway back
about the year 1800 our family name was O'Shannery, and
the folks lived in England, but one day Sean O'S up and
murdered some clunk (who probably deserved it) and fled to
Germany and changed his name to Arnold and I am de-
scended from him—how about that? Struth! My lawyer
brother traced the lineage for us a few years ago, as a legal
matter. Then he wanted to hush it up. Maybe I should too.

Well, at retirement time Wish McNamara was an Irish Catholic, and I was an Irish Protestant, but we was both in the good old USA hence no religious war developed between us neighbors, we just met often and swapped yarns and soda pop, and everything remained hunky-dory. We had different jobs, but even that didn't matter. I was a "crazy writer feller," an un-understandable freak who, faith and begorrah, sat upstairs over his patio' in a lonely office all day and pecked at a silly typewriter instead of doing some respectable he-man labor. Whereas Wish—as I now look back on those decades—was an early version of the distinguised Mr. Archie Bunker, him who has made such a mark for *all* individualists on a national television comedy series.

Wish McNamara was foreman of a big construction crew. A muscle man. But with brains too—y'understand? He had savvy. Loved everybody, even those he occasionally felt impelled to clout, big 200-pound pot-bellied ape that he was, and still is. And if any one didn't love him back, he clouted that one with his fist and put him back in line. Good sound Irish p-sy-chology. I loved Wish. I didn't dare not to; I weigh only 138 pounds. I guess I still love, even though 400 miles now separate our homes.

Well, all right. So The Boss and The Boys gave Wish a big dinner and a cheap imitation-gold watch and made speeches and drank things and shed tears and shook hands and booted him out of his job and he slunk on home and on Monday mornings at 8 o'clock instead of going routinely to work as he had done for 44 years he slunk onto my patio where I was having a second breakfast cuppa and he slobbered out "Good Mother of God, Arnold, I'm done! I won't last until Saint Swithin's Day. I'll die." Self-pity deluxe.

I forgot just who Saint Swithin was. Maybe he was Celtic too. But no matter; his "Day" was later that month. Depressed old friend Wish was low, low. He was ready to discuss the color of his coffin, the type of funeral preferred, all such.

So there in my patio I cussed him a little, pep-talked him,

got his spirits back up, plied him with coffee and cake and conversation, and soon had him seeing how lucky he was. It took more than an hour, but finally he saw the light.

"You are so right!" he exclaimed at last, nodding emphatically, grinning in high spirits again. Irishmen do have bounce. "I am lucky. I have worked hard all my life, I have earned my right to rest. I am going to enjoy the remainder of my life just doing nothing."

"That's the spirit," I lied to him, exhuberantly.

His property adjoined mine. But because his laboring hours had kept him away from home, his yard and patio were relatively barren, whereas mine across the oleander hedge was all fancied up with trees and shrubs and vines and flowers and even a fountain that was forever getting corroded so as to stop spouting. All in all it was lovely out there back of the home that my Adele and I had built for ourselves and three pretty little daughters.

"GO GET YOUR FAVORITE CHAIR."

I said to Wish, "Go bring your favorite old battered-up canvas chair over here under the shade of my big spreading mulberry tree. Put it right here close to mine." Two old washed-up gents, talking.

My chair was handmade of willow limbs and a fine thick untanned sheepskin. I had made it myself. Learned how decades before when an Old Negro taught me, down on our farm in Texas; we cut the willow limbs from around our fish pond, long and soft and flexible when green, and curved them into an armchair shape, tied with rawhide thongs. Fun! Soft and comfortable—and ugly. Well no; not ugly, picturesque. Nothing good is really ugly, ever. Adele yearned to give it to our garbage man, but never did because I had threatened her with divorce and no alimony if she tried it. The chair Wish brought over looked like something the garbage man had already carried away and he himself had retrieved from the city dump, but it fit his bulging bones and buttocks just as my wooly one comforted my angular frame.

"We will *both* retire," I informed Wish McNamara. "Two old Micks, over the hill, enjoying a long, well-deserved rest. You are tired of bossing laborers, I am tired of battling editors. Both groups are bums at heart. We will quit them."

Grinning, we had shaken hands on it. Clapped each other's shoulders (his clap jarred me, but mine merely brushed him; the big ox). In Spring, Summer and Autumn— said we—and even on sunny winter days of which our town had a super-abundance, the two of us would sit together in the outdoors every day and enjoy cussing out the guv'ment, the non-Christians including all Nazis, wild wimmen, lazy-loafer men, anything else of which we disapproved. What a golden dream it was! One day I would whip up a little lunch for us, next day he would; share and share alike. Our wives could go mind their own business. We were two old fire horses turned out to pasture. We would do absolutely nothing at all. Peace, it was wonderful.

PARADISE REGAINED.

That paradise endured for four days.

Then Aloysius McNamara, retiree, got mad, got up out of that canvas chair, got himself down to a big shopping center, and got himself a fine old-man's job of bossing the Security Force there. A policeman, no less! Big Irishmen make fine policemen. Wish had 10 employees under him, and within six months the wealthy owners of that shopping center said that their crime rate had dropped 90 percent under its former level, and that their stores' total sales had increased.

Typically—one day a goony 19-year-old kid snatched Mrs. Lora Alexander's purse there in the Mall, and ran with it. Jeweler Otto Schneider saw the snatch, and telephoned Wish McNamara in Wish's cubbyhole office out on the vast parking area, describing the culprit.

Old formerly-retired Wish took out after that thief. Run, run run!! The boy had a long knife when Wish cornered him in the trash-garbage area behind the stores. But so what? Wish kicked up unexpectedly, hit the fist holding the knife, which sent the knife into a thorny hedge of pyracantha bushes. In the same motion old Wish grabbed the boy's arm, jerked him off balance, slapped him *pow-pow-pow-pow* back and forth a few times, twisted the arm into a hammer lock and marched him to the cubbyhole Security Office.

By legal rights, Wish should then have radioed the city police and turned the boy in, so that some stupid judge could slap his wrist and release him.

Wish did no such. He put the kid into a car and drove him to his slum-district home. There, Wish discovered a widowed mother who had barely enough money to arrange one meal a day for her children. So Wish gave her a $20 bill to buy food, then took the purse snatcher on back to the shopping center.

"Son," he growled at the boy, "you have just joined my Security Force. Stand up straight. Comb your hair back. Wear this badge. Look proud. Now go out and patrol around those hundreds of cars parked out there.

"If you see any woman loaded with parcels, you tip your cap to her and offer to help tote the parcels. If you see anybody needing any kind of help, you give the help, or pick up the phone on one of those light posts out there and call me. Stay alert. Patrol! Look for customers who have problems, and help solve them—you understand?"

"Y-yes sir. I-I think so." The boy was still a bit disoriented, because a miracle was happening and absorbing it took a bit of doing.

As I write this, that same boy, now aged 25, is First Assistant Security Guard in that huge shopping center, a smiling black gentleman wholly dependable and efficient, who often takes full charge when Wish McNamara elects to go fishing. But most days, old Wish, now slowed by "rheumatics" which you elitists would call arthritis, sits in his cozy little office with radio transmitter in hand and keeps close touch with his officers out there under the black man. *Wish made a second career for himself,* after "retirement."

Aren't people wonderful? I ask you—aren't they? You who are not nearly as old as me and Wish were, are, can make yourself a second career, if you won't like your present one. Have I mentioned that adaptability is important for people past age 35? I meant to! Well then—adapt. Don't just sit there feeling sorry for yourself in a battered old canvas chair; get your carcass up out of there and get going in some endeavor that you enjoy and that is rewarding to yourself and to humanity . . . Am I getting through to you, on this?

Every now and then Wish McNamara and I managed to get together again. What an ecumenical hugging and bopping and handshaking and whooping and laughing takes place! "Old" men? Who's old? Not me nor Wish!

On those occasions Wish always puts on a big act, Irish ham that he is. "We will quit work yet—you just wait!" he rumbles at me. All micks talk too loud. "Not likely the same day, though. You'll quit when I help tote you to the cemetery. Or vicey versy."

I like the vicey versy better.

12

Enjoy Your Eccentricities

At intervals in this book I have used the term "common sense."

But to tell you the truth, I don't much like it.

Long experience tells me that persons who are "common-sensible" are likely to be uncommon bores.

They not only bore you and me and everyone else who has to be around them, they bore the unholy bejabbers out of themselves without realizing it. Any person who is eternally doing "what is sensible and right" turns me off. He does not live a happy, zestful life, he is much too rigid and unforgiving and smugly superior. The doctrine that "common sense" is sacrosanct is poppycock.

Give me the nonconformist; no, not the kooky one, not the violent rebel, but the happy-go-lucky innovative one, the imaginative gent or gal who is never teetotally predictable.

In short, I like "eccentrics." Heavens, I am one of them!

Never in my many decades of living has my routine been very much blueprinted or dictated or circumscribed or for heavens-to-Betsy "organized." But I'll be cow-kicked if I haven't enjoyed every minute of it. Also I seem to love practically everybody, and in turn am loved far beyond my deserving.

These points are extremely important to all of you citizens who would Pursue Happiness in mature manner, beginning at age about 35.

YOUR OWN NORM FOR HAPPINESS

In America we do not cringe before any commissar or policeman. If any officer does knock at our door, we expect him to remove his hat in courteous respect and calmly ask our help in some emergency; he dare not try to hustle us off to some horrid Siberia, or even to some local jail without very positive reason. In short, this is America, and we are a land of eccentrics; of freedom thinkers, who by gosh have both the right and the obligation to work out our own individual forms of happiness, so long as these do not impinge unduly on other people. Magnifico! This comes into full flower when we reach the maturity of middle age or more. Kids *think* they are opting for freedom of thought and action, when usually they are just parading their immaturities. We old heads don't have to do that.

Can you remember the great stage play titled, *You Can't Take It With You?* Its central theme is precisely what I have outlined above; that each of us has an inborn right to Do His/Her Own Thing, within the bounds of reason. This is the great glory of the aging years. After all, sir or madam, you *can't* take your money with you, nor your status, your social prestige or whatever, when you leave this earth. So why attach so much importance to it now, why not relax and do some odd, "eccentric" things that are truly enjoyable?

Which brings up that wonderful old yarn—very true of course, as all my "stories" are—about the eccentric 80-year-old who figured that he *could* take it with him. So, being very wealthy, he placed $1,000,000 in a suitcase and stashed it in the attic of his home, so that when he died he could pick it up on his way to heaven. Good thinking!

Well, of course he did soon die, and the next week his widow was cleaning out the house. Sure enough, she found that suitcase still sitting up there in the attic. Whereupon she exclaimed, "Pshaw, I *knew* he should have put that money in the basement!"

CASCADE OF SILVER

I also know a true story about money. In Las Vegas, Nevada, an old man lived his last 20 years in a mansion with four servants, but no kin or friends. He seemed to be entirely "normal" and nice, quiet, refined. Minded his own business, seemed very happy.

Now *his* Thing was to collect coins. Not rare ones, just coin-of-the-realm, of any issue at all. Not paper money, not stocks and bonds, not real estate, not mortgages or other investments, silver coins! In that desert cesspool-of-gambling, coins for slot machines had become meaningful to the old codger.

All right, so he too up and died dead; people do, you know. Whereupon a close friend of my Adele and me, a highly efficient woman office-manager type with fiscal know-how, was hired to come settle his estate. She was instructed to go through his many files of papers, get everything shipshape and legal for the several charities in his will, also of course for the omnipresent Internal Revenue Service. She found that he had left many nice bequests—but negligible money in banks or elsewhere with which to activate them. So—just another dotty old man. Sad.

But to put the mansion itself on the market, she got to poking around in it. Was it structurally sound? Any termites, rotting timbers and such? She needed to know, for appraisal. Testing, she hit a wooden wall with a hammer—and as planks gave way under interior pressure, out poured a cascade of silver! It took her a week, but she eventually counted $88,000 in silver coins, many of them nickels and dimes, that he had poked through a high-up hole. The old boy had enjoyed extra fun, polishing each coin.

Eccentric? You decide. Something tells me that all of us would have liked the old fellow. Especially when we learn that The Salvation Army, the Red Cross, four churches, and a home for retarded children, inherited his fortune. Other hollow walls also were filled with glistening silver coins. "Common sense," no. Fun, yes.

FRESH GRASS CLIPPINGS AND GOAT'S MILK

Now consider another of the many wonderful old friends who have enriched my life. They help make my point about eccentricities, and they also deserve to be remembered.

This one had that All-American name—Lincoln. No known kin to Abe, he said; although there was a strong facial resemblance, and their ancestors came from the same part of England. This one was named John C, usually just called "J.C." Years ago *The Reader's Digest* paid me a fat fee to travel America and dig up material for a personality profile about J.C. Then I spent long hours with him in person, in fact we were in the same church and close personal friends, until I had to serve one day as a pallbearer for him.

J.C. was the founder-developer of the world's largest electric welding enterprise. It had headquarters in Cleveland, and branches around the world. So be became immensely wealthy. And so, again—he elected to move to sunny Scottsdale, Arizona, sit down and do nothing, as an old washed-up over-the-hill retiree. The same syndrome as that of my other friend Aloysious McNamara (see preceding chapter). Once I heard J.C. tell our Kiwanis Club in a speech that his electric welding company had to pay $23,000,000 in *extra* income taxes for that year; then he removed his glasses and added wryly, "Not many men could afford to pay that much extra tax." An understatement if ever I heard one! Eccentric.

He had more than 100 inventions to his credit; a sort of latter-day Edison. But he had been reared as the son of an impecunious country preacher, so that all through his early years he had been forced to scrimp and save every possible penny for food. Now as an old retiree he *still* felt thrifty. Not chincy-mean, but careful of his money; very generous, but wary of con men and exploiters; never liked to see any waste of money, energy or time.

So there in Scottsdale he took to mowing his own lawn.

Never mind his millions now in the bank, he needed the exercise; besides which, the mowing saved paying somebody two dollars. Meanwhile, just a mile away he had built what probably was America's finest resort hotel, Camelback Inn (owned today by the famed Marriott chain) for a mere $3,000,000 or so; an old-age outlet for him. Meanwhile he had planted himself half a dozen orange trees. So—he would pick a bushel or two of ripe oranges, drive a mile to the kitchen door of Camelback Inn, and *sell* those oranges to the head chef, for another two dollars. He and the chef usually haggled a little; but the chef was no fool, he knew who The Boss was, so he finally came to terms with John C. Lincoln. All very serious, you understand.

Then J.C. became a little too old to push a lawn mower at home, so he and his Helen took to raising fine milk goats. More fun! They could eat down the grass at home. But nanny goats have goatlets—or is the word kids?—so the herd increased, so more and more grass was needed for feed, so multi-millionaire J.C. Lincoln would drive to Camelback Inn when the yard keepers were mowing there and make them put the grass in the trunk of his luxury sedan and he would happily haul that green grass back home and feed it to his nannies, each of whom he knew by name. Thrifty! But there's more. Baby goats—endearing little pets around any home—could not drink all the fine rich food from their mamas' udders, so rich old J.C. took to milking those nannies. And serving it to his multi-millionaire guests and others who streamed through the Lincoln home!

Have you ever swigged a tall, cold glass of nanny goat milk?

It is very nourishing, but—well, it *does* come from goats, and goats are not cows, and tradition is tradition, and imagination plays a big part in appetite and taste, and it does have a unique sort of startling taste. But never mind all that. Your host is tall, happy, smiling, very wealthy John C. Lincoln. So when he opens his refrigerator and pours you out a pint of goat milk, and himself one, and lectures you a little on good health, you won't quibble; you drink the darn stuff down, see.

It was great fun to watch rather snobbish bankers from Cleveland and New York and Phoenix and Los Angeles visit the Lincoln home, and because of fiduciary finagling there on the terrace, have to force down big glasses of goat milk to keep their host happy. I have done just that repeatedly, myself. And seen lesser mortals—if there are any—do the same. Including preachers. Women guests, especially, tended to quail when presented with that milk. But if their husbands need the X jillion dollars at state in the conference here—!

Ah well, may J.C. forever rest in peace. May we fondly remember his odd ways, his abiding smile, his unlimited kindnesses; and the precedents in individualism that he left for us all.

MONEY AND ECCENTRICITY

Sociological studies by experts show that *most* so-called eccentricities are not only harmless but are actually beneficial to the eccentric one and his/her friends. This is true even if you are under age 35. I know a modern woman aged 33, who, for some unknown reason, became highly interested in earthworms—imagine! Well, she pursued it, and within two years had launched an industry. Today she markets small plastic bags of what are called ''worm castings.'' This is merely the finest fertilizer you can ever hope to buy, for potted flowers especially. My own Adele tried it on petunias and azaleas, and brother! I myself was farm reared, you know; so I had and still have some savvy about plant nourishment. But those worm castings, from that ''eccentric'' modern female, are making her a fortune. Let's change the word ''eccentric'' to ''innovative.''

Money is not always involved. I also know a man who goes around a beach town, quietly saying to about six people every day—''Is there some way I could help you? What is your problem? I will keep it confidential, and help if I can.''

Eccentric! Surely so. But the results have been astounding, because by instinct he ferrets out people who do need help, do need friendly Christian counsel. Would you feel at ease, doing that? This gentleman is aged 42.

Even more impressive is the record of Aaron and Dorothy Powers, who are around 50 years of age. It is *so* important that I am writing an entire book about their Christian outreach. Aaron is pastor of the Highland Park Presbyterian Church in Los Angeles, in a socially and economically "depressed" area, meaning that he chose to work with poor people rather than with the socially elite. Unable to have children of their own, he and his Dorothy have taken no fewer than 72 distressed children, and a few adults, into their home, some for permanent adoption, others simply as foster children, for periods of six months to life.

If *that* is eccentricity, then God grant that all of us become eccentrics.

You may ask, "How can Aaron and Dorothy afford to do that? Were they rich people to begin with?"

No, they were not. And I asked Aaron that precise question, one day on the golf course. His reply: "My salary is rather low. I am in debt $3,000 at this moment. But I am not worried, ever. Because—now get this, Oren, and *believe* it!—God always provides. God likes to surprise people. I never know where our needed money will come from, so I don't ask or question. We eat well, we have a big old barny manse with abundant room, we have two cars. And we are suffused with love for one another."

The very next day, somebody unexpectedly sent Aaron a cord of wood for the home fireplace; just dumped it anonymously in his yard. A grocer marked his bill for the month "Paid in Full" and sent that to him. A distinguished judge, from whom Aaron had gotten a little boy in the courtroom, a lad with alcoholic and dope-addict parents, delivered the boy to the manse with his personal check for $2,000. Next Sunday in his pulpit, Aaron laughingly told his people that the bed he and Dorothy slept on had springs and mattress shaped like a hammock and they had to sleep in curves, so they planned to use a little of that money buying themselves a bed. But on the way to the furniture store, they found a drunken bum lying in the gutter. They put him in their car, turned around, took him to their home, bathed him, cut his hair, shaved him, sobered him, fed him, dressed him in clean clothes. "That night," Aaron told the congregation, "our old bed felt more comfortable than ever, so we will keep it." He did not make a "production" of it; made no appeal for help, in fact never makes such an appeal. Just reported an incident.

But on Monday morning, a huge truck rolled into his driveway and workmen unloaded six big expensive doublebed sized mattresses—a gift from one of his parishioners who owned a furniture store.

The Powers duo were so grateful, they threw a "mattress party" and invited all the congregation, along with Adele and me. So on a specified night we all gathered there, sat on those mattresses in shifts, and ate barbecued hot dogs, beans and salad out of paper plates. Then sang popular songs, told jokes, romped with children, and signed a thank-you letter to the furniture man. New mattresses for all the beds in that preacher's home! Wonderful!

Is my point clear? About being "eccentric" as you age along?

You know, of course, that we really *can't* take it with us. We can take only what we have made of our souls. And I have a hunch that Saint Peter will open The Gate quicker for freespirit eccentrics, than he will for the authoritarian nononsense eternally Perfect mortals who apply Up There.

Yes, maybe a lot of people like that are "odd."

Well, the aging Benjamin Franklin was odd, too, messing around with a childish kite. Cranky old Tom Edison was odd; so odd, that when he first captured and reproduced sound he said so what, it will never amount to anything. (He really said that!) Come to think on it, Jesus Christ was another famous oddball, eccentric, nonconformist. Imagine—going around

turning water into wine, feeding multitudes with just a hand-
ful of fish and bread, resurrecting dead folk, all that.

But then he, of course, was still young. Never even reached
middle age as we know it.

13

The Miracle Of Meditation

In developing your *total* personality, guaranteeing that the second half of your life will be better than the first, nothing is more important than what we call "meditation."

Too few people do any real thinking, ever. The tendency is to drift along by habit, letting the brain potential lie dormant. Meditation is the highest level of thinking.

Generally, it is best done alone. No, you need not become self-centered or introspective. But in genuinely helpful meditation—thinking—your wife cannot help you; your husband cannot help you, your children and friends cannot. So, this is your cue to walk out "apart"—just as Christ often did; somewhere close to Nature, any quiet place where you can sit down calmly—and meditate. The results in enriching your life can be utterly astounding.

"Meditation" is somewhat of a new art on the American scene. Oh yes, we all know that Moses and Plato and Socrates and Jesus and surely that high-adrenalin genius who changed his name from Saul to Paul, all meditated. Deeply, too. In fact we can assume that the prehistoric Pithecanthropus Erectus—the slant-headed cave gent whose bust adorns high school classrooms today—at times was prone just to lay down his club, loosen his lionskin sarong, sit on a rock beside a gurgling stream, rest chin on fist and become a model for Rodin's classic masterpiece, *The Thinker*. If old Pithy had *not* done that, we today wouldn't even have the wheel, much less the automobile. We do not know precisely when God put that divine urge to think into man, the ability to meditate.

Perhaps it was in Adam and Eve—though Adam didn't seem to use it very well!

Sadly, we sophisticates of 20th Century A.D. have tended to neglect it, too; or ignore it. We have been too cotton pickin' "busy" in what we have felt was Pursuit of Happiness, to go sit under a tree and meditate. Meanwhile we forget what Happiness really is.

Meditation restores the memory.

In recent years many versions of meditation have been publicized, advertised, exorcised and whatever, forcing it on the American and world consciousness. There is a thing, for example, called "Transcendental" Meditation—whatever that is, and nobody is quite sure. The word *transcendental* has a whole mess of definitions. But generally it means extending over everything, surpassing all else, superior, all-encompassing, even supernatural. Therefore the vaunted Transcendentalism seemed to offer possibilities, as I looked into it for you.

When the guru (he had an impressive beard and a deep-in-the-barrel voice) practitioner then said he would teach me his Meditation technique for $125 as a beginning, I cooled fast.

I am not *about* to pay some clunk $125 to learn me how to go sit under a daggone tree and Think! The thought gets my hackles up. Instead, I am going to re-read some of The Psalms and maybe the Sermon on The Mount, then walk out there, sit quietly and *listen*. I suggest you do the same thing. We can be sure that Somebody will talk to us from on high; and that we will be transcendent in our meditation before we realize it.

POLYSYLLABIFICATION!

Another form of meditative malarky has sort of caught on in America during recent years. It is called existentialism.

That big word may impress some of our more simple-minded and pseudo-intellectual citizens, but you and I need not take it seriously at all. As with transcendentalism, it is not "bad," it just doesn't amount to much. I cannot imagine Christ's using it; *he* told us—authoritatively—that we all had to become as little children. Understand? A modern guru-type "philosopher" said that each person exists as an individual in a purposeless universe. Phooey. I wish that my old East Texas Presbyterian minister in 1912 or so could have heard Jean-Paul Sartre say that! Brother Hornbeak was 6-feet-6-inches of kindliness, and he would have bibled the bejabbers out of Sartre. Jimmy Carter came along in 1976—never mind about any "politics" here—and sort of led us Modern Americans back to those biblical fundamentals in thinking, and until some better basis for upgrading our total personalities than being born again comes along, Jimmy's and Brother Hornbeak's will do.

So okay, then. The most astute psychologists of our day agree that you must do *some kind* of simplified but serious thinkings as you age along. This must not be a specious or spasmodic effort, it must be in earnest, and be reasonably regular; a permanent part of your routine.

Best way is to start with four or five sessions of it, without announcing or "advertising" that you are doing so. Just go out and start thinking about your past, present and future. *Calm* thinking, not the fervid type. Nothing that smacks of self-pity, nor of assessing blame on either yourself or other people. Assessing blame is always the most futile of human endeavors, and certainly this is true in the latter half of our lives. What does it matter, now, whose "fault" it was or is, if any person's life to date has been somewhat less than perfect? You cannot re-run the reel. Yes, you can make a few amends, can do some bits of restitution. But every element of good sense says forget the mistakes and build anew. In your meditation, build less on what has been, and more on what is going to be. The latter, you do have the opportunity and intelligence to control.

Investigative reporters (a new breed of in-depth study groups in recent years) have determined that very, very few people really do *any* kind of earnest meditation; mentally, we just drift. The main reason is—we simply don't know how. And we procrastinate about trying to learn by doing.

THE HOW-TO OF MEDITATING

There are no set rules. You need no special costume or other trappings, no long beard, no Moorish burnoose, no burning incense, no soft background music canned in Hollywood. Meditation is as natural as breathing, and as simple.

Location for it does have some bearing. It would be difficult for anyone to meditate at, say, a football game or a rock concert. It can be and often is done in a church, a monastery, a synagogue. It can be done in the privacy of a bedroom; privacy, mind you; groups of two or two thousand can pray together effectively, but the fine art of meditation—as with most fine arts—is best pursued alone.

Where I live, I can walk down to the seashore each day— and enjoy a Happening. Great waves roar toward me, their tops curling like ostrich plumes. Then they flatten out, subside in noise, finally rustling and whispering like taffeta around my bare toes. There I can commune. There I can plunge in, to wash myself clean both literally and figuratively. Riding the crests, I am always impressed with the majesty of the ocean. Its importance in our lives is beyond reckoning. Neptune? I think that is simply a folk name for God. For only an almighty God can create and rule a roaring sea. I seem to do my best meditative thinking while there on my back (which I can do interminably, without "swimming") staring up at the turquoise sky, the gliding seagulls in their exquisite poetry of motion. In such moments a quiet new inspiration begins to suffuse me, and soon my enthusiasm for work and life in general is renewed. But I can work that same magic elsewhere, too, and so can you.

Thoreau said that "All men live lives of quiet desperation."

He was wrong. He might have been great as a naturalist, but he did not know much about people. Most people live for and by that *in*spiration, and we develop it best in our meditation. It is one of the unearned mercies of God; a mystery gift, of infinite value and potential.

An ordinary tree (though every tree on earth is really *extraordinary!*) can be a first focal point for meditation. So can a wild flower. So can the green grass. Grass? It is a marvel beyond our ability to understand. It is not merely beautiful, it sustains the most valuable animal on earth, the cow. Or what about the stars, the sun? The moon? It lost much of its glamor when we put men on it, but even so—beauty! A grand Japanese lantern, floating there in our skies, a stimulus to our imaginations.

There will be times, of course, when you will need to go apart and "think out" problems, perhaps very acute ones concerning health, money, family crisis, personal matters, emergencies of any kind. But for even those harsher moments, a *preliminary* period of meditation is advisable, and next-to-Nature somewhere is the best setting for it.

Perhaps the best way to begin any meditation is to tense your muscles—all of them—hold your breath a few seconds, then just let go. Exhale. Become totally "loose" of body, free of tension.

Next—a short whispered prayer for guidance, a petition that lays your soul bare and invites divine help. Sit still, physically and mentally, for a few minutes. Listen! Listen to the meadowlarks, if any; the mocking birds; the doves; the little sounds of Nature. Very soon, you will be "listening" with your mind, your psyche, your soul. And new realizations will dawn inside you; new understandings. Experience this phenomenon just once, and you will never forget it. You will regain confidence, and poise, and self-assurance, and humility, all in one. Then you go back to any emergency and deal with it.

Such is the very ultimate in meditation. Meditation is not some vague "religion," of itself; rather it is a wholly natural need and craving in all of us of every religion. Certainly it is the very essence, the undergirding, of Christianity. It is re-creative; an *appreciative* approach to living. Appreciative!

Can you grasp the importance, the majesty, of that word? This is especially true for men and women at middle age and after, those with maturing minds.

Thus it becomes our richest late-blooming blessing.

14

Rebuttal For America's
Merchants Of Despair

Very soon, now, we are going to adjourn this meeting, so that you can use your new mental notes toward enriching your life. But there is one last consideration that I must lay before you. Knowing you to be intelligent—I keep harping on that!—I truly realize that you are concerned not only with your personal welfare and that of your loved ones, but God bless you, you also are concerned with the welfare of America as a whole. And America, need I tell you, in recent years has seemed to be in deep, deep trouble, at least in many persons' thinking. This attitude can indeed affect the upgrading of your personal and family life.

So—

It is entirely possible—indeed it is definite—that the calamity howlers in America are wrong.

It is high time that the rest of us challenge them, not in ostrich-like optimism or backbiting anger, but in terms of calm reasoning and common sense.

Almost hourly, those howlers issue lists of our national imperfections and failures. I could do that myself. I am furious about the power of tenure, the dictatorship of Labor leaders, the self-pampering money-grabbing habits of many Senators and Congressmen, the wasteful "foreign aid" expenditures, the fact that every third adult you encounter on the street today is sucking the government teat, nourished on the milk of taxation. Shame on them, and all their ilk. You and I and every person in America, newborn babies included, owe about $40,000 on the national indebtedness and there is no possible end of inflation except repudiation, and—

Don't get me started! I will roar all over the landscape. And yes I do urge you to sound off, to use your ballot and your personal influence in correcting the national faults.

But truth is, a great deal of this kind of talk is simply from unwitting merchants of despair. Millions of "good" though fearful, faithless folk reiterate their propaganda of doom.

Melodramatically, these offer evidence: "Just look at the murders, the muggings, the holdups and the burglaries, the student rebellions, the decadence of morality in general," usually adding the snapper that "crime in general is at an all-time high."

DON'T YOU BELIEVE IT!

The cold truth is—*there is less crime in America today than at any other time in our history!*

True, there is more *total* outlawry, because there is more total of almost everything. With so many more people, it would be astounding if we did *not* have a volume increase in badness as well as goodness.

But the *percentage* of crime is definitely down!

For proof, you can begin with our nation's preconception period in history. Life under England's Elizabeth I was hellish. No honest man of means dared walk the streets of London without a bodyguard. Killings and thievery by night were routine. So many travelers were murdered and robbed that Her Majesty ordered all trees and shrubbery cut back 100 feet from every highway, hoping to lessen the chances of ambush. It didn't work; brigands simply blocked the highway with logs, and they did this despite many public hangings and many lifetime sentences in horrible prisons.

In the new Colonies on our shores, a blunderbuss, a knife, a sword, even a hand axe, were literally necessities of life for any person venturing more than a few yards from his home.

All through the Revolutionary period—and afterward in the Federal era—crime on the streets was exceeded only by dishonesty and graft in high places or by outlaws on country roads. It was a dog-eat-dog era. Most of our citizens then could not read or write, hence in their ignorance they could not defend themselves from confidence men, counterfeiters, grafters, slickers in general. Theirs was largely a *physical* life; shoot first or be shot, strike first or be killed.

In the sophisticated decades of the early 1800's, when America was maturing, violence was so rampant that virtually every male over age 14 had to carry a firearm almost everywhere he went. Doors and windows barred at night, the loaded rifle over the mantel, the constant need for alertness and defense—these, with policing almost nonexistent, were a way of life, accepted everywhere as inevitable, Psychologically, this was one reason why North and South could spring to Civil War with such bravado; our people's minds were conditioned to violence.

RECONSTRUCTION HORROR

We also know that Reconstruction in the South was anything but calm. It was, most tragically, exploitation, again with violence at every turn, so much so that sheer despair drove thousands of would-be gentlefolk westward, seeking any life not quite so vicious. But then again, in St. Louis, Denver, Laramie, El Paso, Tucson, Seattle, "Frisco," and in that new town ironically named "The Angels," what was the order of the day?

Violence! Crime!

Every man and older boy wore a gun, often two. Survival required it; not style nor show-off mores, just sheer survival.

You think that our TV yarns are exaggerated? You consider Matt Dillon, Wyatt Earp and their colleagues as purely fictional, overdrawn by dishonest writers in our time? Not on your tintype! You have not read your social history. The period sidearms and quick-draw attitudes were imperative. The saloon, the bawdy house, the stagecoach robberies, the very atmosphere of outlawry as a routine part of living, in many areas continued right on down through the year 1900 and into this "enlightened" century.

But do you carry a rifle today, sir? Do you even own one?

Do you wear a pistol on your thigh, a knife in your belt, a Derringer up your sleeve, when you step out to the neighborhood bar at night?

Can your wife get into her stagecoach (eight cylinders, not eight horses) and drive alone, happily, safely, from Tucson 400 miles to Los Angeles, with no thought of criminal danger? (My wife does precisely that, in modern routine.) Can she go to church alone, to the grocery, to visit Aunt Susan on the country farm?

Can your daughter go to college with the feeling that she need have no fear, that she can shrug off those kooks in too-long hair and no shoes who sometimes cause violence, smile pityingly at them and get on with her education? She couldn't have in 1880.

Of course! Ours is not an era of violence, not even remotely so, if we measure 1980 against 1880.

As for the headline makers, the disorders on campuses in recent years—keep in mind that America has about 3,000 colleges and universities. Despite all the hullabaloo about Kent and Berkeley and others, despite the few tragic deaths also, *fewer than five percent* of America's students have been involved in any form of protest or strife.

Typically, one university, excited by threats of violence and by some actual vandalism, counted the maurauders and found only 90. But the total enrollment there exceeded 22,000 and most of these were openly disdainful of the 90, quietly going about their business of seeking an education. The vast majority did not make the headlines.

The same types of alarmists also keep harping on a "new sexual revolution" among our youth; they see an extension of juvenile delinquency everywhere. But one authoritative torpedo will sink that cherished misconception. Dr. James Elias, the distinguished sociologist at Indiana University, recently said categorically that, "There is no sex revolution taking place among our youth in America today. The present teenagers are no more promiscuous than their parents were." Come to think on it, gentle reader—just how promiscuous, were you, in your own teens, and what about today? I'm just asking!

Today's teenagers use sex language more freely than did their elders, but to say that they are running rampant and are controlled by lust is—declared Dr. Elias—"not supported by data." Youth's wildness has been created largely by sensational writers and other alarmists who have not bothered to gather facts.

"Delinquency" doubtless began with young Cain. Certainly The Prodigal Son was nothing more than a hippie-delinquent, at first. And a Sumerian tablet in the museum at the University of Pennsylvania tells about a significant case of juvenile delinquency. Words on it are those of a harassed father addressing his son: *"Why are you loafing around? Go on back to school, son; do your assigned work. When you have finished that and done what your teacher says, don't just walk the streets, but come to me. Do you understand me?"*

That was papa speaking, not in 1979 but 3,000 years ago!

Albert G. Hess, a distinguished authority on social history, cites endless shocking instances of juvenile crime in the 17th, 18th and 19th centuries, ranging from murder and arson through gambling, drinking and general gangsterism. He says that in the U.S.A. around 1900 boys fighting on the streets or playground were viewed with calm amusement by adult males. Delinquency was expected, accepted. Still another sociologist, Walter W. Meek, recently said, "The reported surge of crime in recent years seems to be a myth. In fact it appears that so-called 'crime waves' can be created in the minds of the public by police reporting techniques."

That pointed a finger right at the crux of the matter—our new, modern *awareness* of crime.

BANDITS!

Technical communication today can be called virtually perfect, yet improvements even here will be made. About one century ago, a stagecoach out West was held up, its $50,000 in gold stolen, its passengers murdered. Weeks had to pass before any publication of that news was made, and then it totaled only two inches in an obscure weekly newspaper. Months had to pass before many parts of America learned of President Lincoln's assassination. Within 30 minutes after President Kennedy was shot, the horror had shocked people in every corner of the globe.

"But that speed in sending out the news is only a part of it," said the distinguished psychiatrist, Dr. Karl Menninger. "The sad part is the reiteration. We hear the reports again and again, the news media constantly repeating them. I think there is much more talk about crime than there is crime itself."

The old journalistic tradition that bad news is what readers prefer probably always was fallacious, but it has compounded the felony here. We become so steeped in crime talk, so brainwashed with pessimism by viewing with alarm, that we have tragically lost our ability to point with pride. Such is the summation of the sociologists.

The felony is further compounded by—of all people—the police themselves, the F.B.I. officials included, and by their unwitting, unintentional henchmen, the clergymen. But pointing up the *bad* things in life is their trade. They are hired to do precisely that, and even though in the process they brainwash themselves, we could not let them change. Up to a point we need their doleful harpings, in order to get adequate appropriations to maintain any police force at all and in order to keep us aware of our sins.

We Americans do need to remember the shame of Mr. Kennedy's assassination. Yet we must also remember that 19th century presidents faced even more prevalent dangers. During the Jackson administration, Vice-President Van Buren felt obliged to preside over the august United States Senate itself with a brace of pistols under his coat. Can you imagine today's Vice-President's doing that?

ENDLESS THREATS

There were so many threats against Abe Lincoln that the Pinkerton Detective Agency had to be hired to guard him, and ultimately failed. Grant also was on John Wilkes Booth's death list that night, but just happened to decline Mr. Lincoln's invitation to Ford Theater. We know that Garfield and McKinley were assassinated.

We reflect that Teddy Roosevelt was shot in Milwaukee in 1912, and that in 1932 a spray of bullets hit Franklin Roosevelt's car, killing Chicago mayor Anton Cermak and wounding four others. We recall that Harry Truman was shot in Blair house while guards ordered him away from a window.

So after all, Mr. Kennedy's death does not tag our modern era as one of unprecedented criminality, not even when abetted by the deaths of Martin Luther King and Senator Robert F. Kennedy. We must remind ourselves that the politics of assassination is at least as old as Julius Caesar and that America from its very beginning had much more violence than it has today.

"Due to our fantastic increase in total human knowledge, and our frantic efforts to adapt to it," said Dr. Edward Lindaman not long ago, as a distinguished space scientist and churchman and college president, "we have many new problems in the late 1970's. But our problems are man-made. Therefore they can and will be solved by man."

I like that summation. The truth is—somebody or something has *always* been out to "get" America, planning and hoping to destroy it; the English twice, the French, the Spaniards, the Mexicans, the Germans twice, the Italians, the Japanese, the Russian Communists, the Confederate Rebels, or surely the nuclear bomb, the Pentagon people, the bureaucrats, the this and the that, on and on *ad infinitum ad nauseam.*

But here we are, with Old Glory still flying.

Here we are, with our churches and schools prospering.

Here we are, with unprecedented industry and commerce, and with the money savings of our people at an all-time high. Here we are, a truly affluent society, teeming with life and love and derring-do. Despite all our imperfections and woes, nothing is going to "get" us! *Nothing!* Because we are—for the first time in human history—one nation *under God.* We say that, and we mean it. We believe it. We are trying hard to live up to it.

* * *

So now is a good time to adjourn this meeting. On a note of upbeat optimism. On the sure promise that each of us individually can indeed improve not only the quality of our personal and family lives, but the total life of our country. We can leave our children a heritage of deep spiritual faith and power.

God bless.

Notes

Notes